# Against Decolonisation

# Against Decolonisation

## Campus Culture Wars and the Decline of the West

DOUG STOKES

polity

First published in 2023 by Polity Press

Polity Press
65 Bridge Street
Cambridge CB2 1UR, UK

Polity Press
111 River Street
Hoboken, NJ 07030, USA

IISBN-13: 978-1-5095-5422-5 (hardback)
ISBN-13: 978-1-5095-5423-2 (paperback)

A catalogue record for this book is available from the British Library.

Library of Congress Control Number: 2023931486

Typeset in 11 on 14pt Warnock Pro
by Cheshire Typesetting Ltd, Cuddington, Cheshire
Printed and bound in Great Britain by TJ Books Ltd, Padstow, Cornwall

For further information on Polity, visit our website: politybooks.com

# Contents

Introduction                                                          1

1 Identity politics, decolonisation and social theory       16

2 Racism on campus                                               35

3 Moral panic and illiberalism in universities              54

4 History reclaimed                                                80

5 Accounting for 'wokery'                                        112

Conclusion: The future of the West?                        136

*Notes*                                                                151
*Index*                                                                187

# Introduction

With the shocking killing of George Floyd in America in 2020 and the rise of the Black Lives Matter movement (BLM), global awareness has been raised about the ongoing injustice of racism. In the US alone, 14,000 protesters were arrested on BLM marches. President Joe Biden captured the sentiment well. He argued that Floyd's death had more of an impact than that of the civil rights leader, Martin Luther King. 'Dr King's assassination did not have the worldwide impact that George Floyd's death did.'[1] The legacy of racism and structural inequality for non-white minorities is now said to be one of the world's principal ethical challenges. The USA's very political DNA has been denounced by its senior leaders. Americans must 'acknowledge that we are an imperfect union – and have been since the beginning', argued Linda Thomas-Greenfield, US Ambassador to the United Nations. The 'original sin of slavery [has] weaved white supremacy into our founding documents and principles'.[2]

Biden's administration has instituted an ambitious 'whole-government equity agenda' to address inequality. On his first day in office, Biden signed the 'Advancing Racial Equity and Support for Underserved Communities' act, a 'generational

commitment that will require sustained leadership and part-
nership with all communities'. It is designed to tackle 'the
enormous human costs of systemic racism, persistent poverty,
and other disparities'.[3] Vice-President Kamala Harris explained
that US citizens will all now 'end up in the same place' and thus
ensure equal outcomes for everybody. Without this change
and transformation, the West's ethical trajectory will remain
compromised and social justice will not be realised.

In response, many parts of American society are undergoing
radical change, even those generally considered to be the most
conservative. For example, the US Navy's new fealty pledge
states that service personnel must 'invest the time, attention
and empathy required to analyse and evaluate Navy-wide
issues related to racism, sexism, ableism and other structural
and interpersonal biases'.[4]

Drawing on academic theories, especially 'critical race
theory', corporate America is also pursuing a new agenda of
Equality, Diversity, Inclusion (EDI) to address what is said to
be lingering forms of 'white privilege' and 'whiteness'. In this
pursuit, liberal forms of anti-racism, captured most notably by
Martin Luther King's insistence on the importance of character over colour, are being abandoned.

The new anti-racism openly advocates the importance of
identity over the individual and, increasingly, the collective
guilt of white people. Yale's Claudia Rankine explained that
those in the West are 'inside a culture that's dedicated to
whiteness and its dominance over other people because white
people have been socialised to believe that they are superior,
better-looking, smarter'.[5]

The rot is said to be so deep that Stanford's Social Innovation
Review argued that even the standards of professionalism are
'defined by white supremacy culture – or the systemic, institu-
tionalized centering of whiteness'. An alleged lack of diversity
at the top of corporate America is taken as indicative of these
trends of structural racism and 'whiteness'.[6] Most American

multinationals have now adopted these ideas. For example, the world's largest asset manager is BlackRock, with US$10 trillion in assets under management in 2022, and now insists on diversity targets for the companies in which it holds shares.[7]

The global dominance of American culture means that the cultural effects of this new illiberal American 'anti-racism' has had a global impact. BLM protests occurred in sixty countries and every continent, even including Antarctica. As Greenfield argued, just 'look at the way the Black Lives Matter movement spread . . . What took hold in the streets of Minneapolis made it to Monrovia, and Madrid, and London, and Sydney, and Berlin, and Cape Town; Stockholm, and Rio de Janeiro, and Tokyo, and on, and on, and on'. These protests are necessary, she argued, as 'in today's world' every society is racist.[8] As such, corporate America and the US government is increasingly wedded to the global export of a worldview predicated around the centrality of identity, the ubiquity of racism and the morally compromised nature of Western civilisation.

The justified disgust at Floyd's killing also helped energise a movement in the UK to address what was said to be a similar history of racial injustice and the legacy effects of discrimination. It was captured symbolically by the toppling of the Bristol-based statue of the slave trader Edward Colston.[9] The protests also targeted other prominent figures from British history said to be tarnished with the evil of racism including Winston Churchill, Oliver Cromwell and Horatio Nelson. Even a statue of the Indian independence leader, Mahatma Gandhi, was targeted and sprayed with the word 'racist'. Demonstrators also attacked the Cenotaph in London, a memorial to the over a million British war dead, including those fighting Hitler's genocidal racism.[10]

From the Archbishop of Canterbury's declaration of the need to remove depictions of a white Jesus to investigations as to why the British countryside is racist, British institutions, like American ones, are undergoing a process of transformation in a desire to be more equitable and to create what are said to be genuinely 'anti-racist' institutions. The call to 'decolonise' British history and its institutions has become one the most important ways to acknowledge the alleged legacy effects of transatlantic slavery. Even King Charles argued that the history of transatlantic slavery should be given the same national level of importance as the Holocaust.[11] How accurate is this characterisation of racism in the US and the UK?

## Racism in America?

The shocking killing of George Floyd reinforced a dominant perception of systemic anti-black racism in American policing. Many have 'concluded that a structural or institutional bias against people of color, shaped by long-standing racial, economic, and social inequities, infects the criminal justice system', argues New York University's Brennan Centre. As a result, these 'systemic inequities can also instil implicit biases – unconscious prejudices that favor in-groups and stigmatise outgroups – among individual law enforcement officials, influencing their day-to-day actions while interacting with the public'.[12]

When asked, over half of Americans with Left-Liberal political views estimated that police killed 1,000 or more unarmed black men in 2019. The actual number was thirteen, according to the leading database on police killings.[13] In the same year, those with liberal to very-liberal political views estimated the proportion of black men killed by the police to be 56% and 60%, respectively, when the actual figure is 24.9%.[14]

When we examine the data, we must control for two crucial variables: demographics and the social contexts of police interactions. The most recent census data for 2020 show that the US is now 57.8% white, 18.7% Hispanic, 12.4% black and 6% Asian. Despite only comprising 12.4% of the population,

African Americans make up 53% of known homicide offenders in the US and commit about 60% of robberies.[15] The Bureau of Justice Statistics showed that in 2021 the 'share of violent incidents involving black offenders (29%) was greater than the population percentage of black persons (12%)'.[16] FBI data show that black or African Americans comprised 44% of all violent offenders in 2021 (compared with 43% of the white population, including the sizable Hispanic population).[17] Of victims, the black or African American population comprised the most significant victim group too, at 38%.

When examining police–citizen interactions, especially those that lead to fatalities, the social context is thus critical. The kinds and prevalence of crimes will be the leading indicator of police interaction in what will likely be high-stress and perilous situations where violence would be statistically far more likely (e.g. homicides, violent crime). Moreover, given this higher prevalence, another key metric in the debate on police–civilian violence is the rate at which firearms are used in those interactions, and thus where there is a higher probability of fatality. What do the data show?

A major study concluded that in areas of relative deprivation, police–citizen encounters were actually 'more likely to result in a police fatality than in a citizen fatality'. Guns were 'significantly more likely to be used by citizens involved in police fatalities'; that helps explain 'why the odds of police lethal victimisation, relative to police use of force, increased in more disadvantaged areas'.[18] The latest data on police killed nationally by felons show that between 2010 and 2019, white offenders killed a total of 303 officers. Black offenders killed 199. As such, of the 537 total murders of police officers between 2010 and 2019, white offenders were responsible for 56% of all murders, and black offenders for 37%. When controlling for demographic factors, black Americans are thus disproportionately responsible for police murders in often highly violent encounters.[19]

Despite this, a leading multifactor study concluded that there is 'little evidence that black citizens are more likely than white citizens to be fatally shot by police nationally'.[20] The authors continue that when examining police–citizen interactions, appropriate benchmarks must be used to understand racial disparities. 'Journalists, advocacy groups, and politicians continue to use the general population benchmark to suggest that the police disproportionately target minorities for deadly force. Framing the issue as one involving racial bias not only misleads but polarises police officers and citizens who want reform.'[21] As such, there is a pervasive implicit bias narrative in relation to American policing but this 'hypothesised relationship between the decision to shoot and suspect race was not supported' by a growing body of major research surveys.[22]

Despite these real-world variables, unarmed black fatalities at the hands of the American police generate nine times as many news search results as white victims.[23] This perhaps confirms a powerful media narrative of structural racism across American policing and society more generally. An admittedly simple test for the ubiquity of this narrative is that while the name of George Floyd is now known around the world, the name of Tony Timpa is largely unknown. Timpa died in almost identical circumstances to Floyd, the crucial difference being that he was white.[24] Since Floyd's death, Edward Bronstein was killed in nearly similar circumstances too, but again, is barely known and is white.[25]

The data on hate crime are similarly counterintuitive. For example, in 2019, race was reported for 6,406 known hate-crime offenders. Of these offenders, 52% were white and comprised 58% of the American population. However, 23.9% of American hate crimes were committed by black Americans despite being only 12.4% of the American population.[26] 2020 figures confirm this. White Americans committed 55% of hate crimes and black Americans 21%.[27]

The dominant narrative of racist white police officers randomly gunning down innocent and unarmed black men is false. Most police killings occur in situations of extreme violence, with the higher level of relative deprivation in an area meaning a higher probability of a police officer being murdered by an armed citizen. When controlling for population size, the police are three times more likely to be murdered by black felons than white felons. To the extent that committing a racially motivated hate crime is a proxy for racism, American blacks are twice as racist as American whites.

None of this is discussed to lessen the legacy of racism in America's history or its likely ongoing effects. Moreover, black Americans are more likely to be deeply concerned about criminal violence, which is unsurprising, given that black Americans are much more likely to be victims of violent crime. Multiple variables will feed into the data above, including poverty, education, family background and culture, all of which intersect in complex ways to shape human agency.

However, the key point is the jarringly counter-intuitive disconnect between the dominant media narrative and reality. More importantly, the moral power of this narrative has gone global, and is now being used to transform the politics, culture and institutions not just of the US but also of the UK, given the historically close connections between the two nations.

## Is the UK systemically racist?

Beyond America, what is the reality in the UK and is it a structurally racist society that needs to be decolonised and undergo radical transformation? Like the US media, the British media has pushed a narrative of ubiquitous racism, xenophobia and discrimination that is allegedly prevalent across the UK. A major study found that between 2010 and 2020, 'terms such as racism and white supremacy in popular UK media outlets increased on average by 769% and 2,827%, respectively'. The report continues that mentions 'of prejudice have also become far more prominent in the BBC, the UK's leading public service outlet. From 2010 to 2020, mentions in BBC content of terms suggestive of racism have increased by over 802% . . . hate speech (880%), . . . or slavery (413%).'[28]

What do those data show? In 2019, the European Union conducted one of the most extensive surveys across the European continent. Its report, *Discrimination in the European Union*, showed that the United Kingdom is one of the least racist societies in Europe; a continent already characterised by extensive anti-discrimination laws and norms, and that partially explains the mass legal and illegal migration from across the world to the continent, especially to the UK. Why would any non-European risk their lives, or move thousands of miles to start a life in a deeply racist hellhole?

On working with a colleague from a different ethnicity, 89% of the British population were comfortable, with 5% either indifferent or did not know. Italy, a mature and developed European democracy, stood at only 56% being comfortable. On being comfortable with the highest political position in the land occupied by somebody from a different ethnic origin or skin colour, the UK scored 88%. This was reflected in the 2022 leadership contest in the UK's Conservative party, where Kemi Badenoch, a black woman of Nigerian ancestry, was the clear favourite among the party's membership, a party regularly portrayed as being xenophobic and racist by its political opponents. At the time of writing, the UK's Prime Minister is Rishi Sunak, whose parents are of Indian descent.

Perhaps more important, and illustrative of how deep anti-discrimination norms have become embedded in British society, 86% of those surveyed reported that they would be comfortable with their children being in a loving relationship with a black person.[29] This is reflected in the data. The last British census data available at the time of writing was

conducted in 2021.[30] It showed that 3% of the British population were mixed race, one percentage point up from the 2011
census that was double from the 2001 census. Research by
Alita Nandi and Lucinda Platt suggests the figure could be
three times as high. If correct, mixed-race people are a more
significant proportion of the population than any other minority ethnic group.[31]

The study above confirms data from an earlier and similarly extensive 2016 European Union Agency for Fundamental
Rights study. It was based on face-to-face interviews with
25,515 respondents with different ethnic minority and immigrant backgrounds across 28 EU member states. While people
of black African descent faced 'widespread and entrenched
prejudice and exclusion' across the EU, the UK had one of the
lowest reported levels of race-related harassment and violence
in the twelve-country study. The highest violence rates were
reported in Finland (14%), closely followed by Austria and the
Republic of Ireland (13%). The figure among UK respondents
was 3%.[32]

Across nearly every measure, the UK was the least racist
and discriminatory country in Europe. A clear majority of 59%
of respondents stated that discrimination was rare to non-
existent in the UK. For African migrants to the UK, only 6%
reported being discriminated against because of their ethnic
origin over twelve months; 0% when looking for housing; 3%
when in contact with their children's schools.[33]

The non-discriminatory nature of the UK shows up in education and earnings too. For example, at our most selective
universities, only 5% of disadvantaged young people enrol
compared with the national average of 12%. Part-time students
from lower-income backgrounds have dropped by a massive
42% over the past six years. The Office for National Statistics
(ONS) figures show that the historically low entry rate into
higher education of white pupils from state schools has been
this way since 2006. The most significant increase in entry

rates between 2006 and 2018 was among black pupils, from 21.6% to 41.2%; the smallest increase was among white pupils, from 21.8% to 29.5%.[34] In contrast, the latest ethnic data show that 38.7% of white pupils went to university, whereas mixed pupils stood at 47.6%, black pupils at 59.9%, and Asian pupils at 64.3% and Chinese pupils 80.9%.[35]

At Oxford, often held up as a beacon of privilege, 24.6% of its 2021 intake were black or minority ethnic students. This confirms an annual trend of upward and significant BME[36] student enrolment (for example, in 2017, BME students admitted were 17.8%). This reflects a broader trend across British universities. The 2019 data show that the proportion of 19- to 25-year-olds across the UK was 80.6% white and 19.4% BME. However, BME students made up almost 29% of the total intake at British universities in the same year, including over 25% at the elite Russell Group.[37] These educational disadvantages have significant real-world effects. The Office for National Statistics data show that Chinese, Indian, and mixed or multiple ethnicity employees all have higher median hourly pay than white British employees, with Chinese employees earning 30.9% more than white British employees.[38]

Tellingly, a child on free school meals is the leading indicator of deprivation, but this does not impact all ethnic groups equally. In terms of progression among young men, 67% of Chinese, 54% of Indian, 53% of Bangladeshi, 52% of black African, and 24% of black Caribbean on free school meals progress to higher education. White British men? At just 13%, they are the least likely group to study at university after those from traveller backgrounds.

A Parliamentary report noted that in 2018/19, just 53% of Free School Meal (FSM) eligible white British pupils met the expected development standard at the end of the early years foundation stage; one of the lowest percentages for any disadvantaged ethnic group.[39] The trends have seemingly become so entrenched that the UK Parliament's Education Select

Committee commissioned a report in 2021 to examine the decades-long disadvantages of white working-class kids entitled 'The Forgotten: How White Working-Class Pupils Have Been Let Down, and How to Change It'. It found that the 'proportion of white British pupils who were FSM-eligible starting higher education by the age of nineteen in 2018/19 was 16%, the lowest of any ethnic group other than travellers of Irish heritage and Gypsy/Roma' with one of the key reasons being a 'failure to address low participation in higher education'.[40]

In what is little more than a form of progressive political hypochondria, the UK's exit from the European Union (Brexit) was also mistakenly portrayed as a xenophobic or racist reaction to non-white immigration and has formed a key part of the narrative that the UK is a racist country.

However, in terms of post-Brexit visas, all the highest groups granted skilled work visas originate outside the European Union. In 2021, 'Indian nationals account for over two-fifths (42%) of all skilled work visas granted. There was a large increase in skilled work visa grants to Nigerian nationals, which more than doubled (+108%) to 8,646 in September 2021. Compared to 2019, Nigerian nationals saw the greatest increase in skilled work visa grants, increasing by 149% (+5,173).'[41] Almost three-quarters (72%) of the initial decisions in 2021 were grants of asylum, humanitarian protection or alternative forms of leave, representing the highest number since 1990.[42] In 2021, there were 48,540 asylum applications to the UK, the highest number since 2003. Despite this, and as the *Financial Times*' extensive data set shows, between '2016 and 2019, the number of immigrants to the UK was broadly unchanged, yet the share of Britons concerned about immigration plummeted from almost half to one in seven'.[43]

More recent polling by ICM Unlimited in January 2021 found that 62% of black British people considered their British national identity to be important – only marginally lower than the more comprehensive general population figure of 64%.

The British Police Service is one of Britain's most vilified public institutions. As part of their adaptation to the post-George Floyd era, they released an 'anti-racist' action plan in May 2022.[44] However, the Police Service enjoys overwhelming support from ethnic minorities. ONS data show that the UK's Chinese, Bangladeshi, Indian and black African demographic have a higher confidence level in their local police force in 2019 than white British people, at over 75%.[45]

While eliminating all racism and discrimination is impossible and, where it raises its ugly head, it should always be tackled robustly, the above-mentioned trends are very clear and apparent. On the one hand, we have a dominant cultural and political narrative that portrays the West and the UK as endemically racist. Following the killing of George Floyd and the intensification of American cultural and political trends in the UK, this narrative of racial moral panic has grown incredibly powerful. It has helped shape British politics and, as we shall see in later chapters, is leading to profound changes across British institutions.

On the other hand, the data show that many ethnic minorities earn more money, have better educational outcomes, and attend universities in greater per capita numbers than the white majority. The UK is not only one of the least racist societies on earth, as evidenced by the remarkable success of its ethnic minorities, which itself is the result of decades of institutional efforts to integrate and welcome minorities, but it remains an open, tolerant and welcoming country, even after Brexit, which is mistakenly portrayed as xenophobic and racist in origin.

## The book's key arguments

This book seeks to explore this puzzle. On the issues of race, identity and equality in the UK, how do we explain the extraordinary contrast between the reality of a successful multi-racial liberal democracy and the dominant narrative of grievance and racial discord that is now leading many British institutions to undergo a process of 'decolonisation'? Nowhere is this more pronounced than in the university system, where these ideas have germinated and spread across British institutions.

In the next chapter, I examine the Cold War shift in Left social theory from a Marxian focus on political economy and class to a postmodern focus on culture and identity. This shift was occasioned by the almost total failure of revolutionary Marxism to inspire ordinary people in the advanced capitalist economies during the Cold War and a subsequent transfer of political hope to third world revolutionary movements. The politics of race and decolonisation were further developed as part of the cultural turn of Left social theory that rejected the materialism of Marxism, championed judgemental relativism and adopted a strategy of the deconstruction of Western civilisation, itself seen as a racist and oppressive construct.

Chapter 2 shows how these ideas have now been adopted across the British university system, especially after George Floyd's killing. British universities have been accused of being systemically racist and guilty of reinforcing unequal outcomes for ethnic minorities, including differential degree outcomes and staff and student numbers. One of the ways to address these alleged unequal outcomes is to undergo a decolonisation process and decentre white, Eurocentric curriculums from our centres of learning. By doing so, universities and European civilisation more generally can begin to atone for slavery, colonialism, and the legacies of these forms of historical oppression. These ideas have been adopted by university leaders and are leading to widespread change on British campuses, and culture and politics more generally.

Chapter 3 then examines the arguments used to sustain this radical transformation of British universities and culture. I show that the arguments of those calling for the decolonisation of British universities are demonstrably wrong. All the available data show universities are incredibly diverse, as is British society. Instead, UK universities have become consumed by a racial moral panic that has accelerated illiberal and authoritarian trends on British campuses, infantilised students, and threatened the keystone value of academic freedom throughout the UK. Even though the UK is one of the least discriminatory societies on earth, there has been an exponential growth of academic sub-fields around the themes of social justice and the alleged ubiquity of prejudice.[46] This has significant implications for the future of Britain and how it understands its identity and place in the world.

Chapter 4 examines the history used to support the claims of the decolonisation movement. I call for a reclamation of history and science. Rather than decolonisation, we should return to rational adjudication, academic freedom and scientific realism. These values have helped propel humanity forward and allow us to fairly interrogate Britain's history. I show that slavery and colonialism have been common throughout human history. Britain helped end slavery, including that of various African slave kingdoms. The claim that all white British citizens are collectively racially guilty for the sin of slavery is morally repugnant and is itself a form of historically illiterate racism.

Chapter 5 relates the decolonisation of British universities to deeper shifts in the politics of the West. A new technocratic Professional Managerial Class (PMC) has emerged under globalisation that secures hegemony through advancing a politics of vulnerability and the bureaucratic corralling of moralising coalitions around identity issues. The 'woke' intersectionalism championed by corporations and PMC elites fits an era geared towards forms of supranational governance in a flat, post-national moral economy. Those who reject these values are portrayed as backward, denigrating their political agency. Absent a return to pluralism, tolerance and fairness, the politics of the Anglophone West will become more divisive and broken.

In concluding the book, I argue that while far from perfect, the Western-led liberal international order has helped transform humanity for the better. The Anglophone world's culture wars have profound geopolitical consequences. The desire to decolonise the Anglophone West and the adoption of identity politics by political and cultural elites are suicidal moves in the context of rising illiberal and authoritarian 'civilisational states' like China. Human freedom and progress are not the natural order of things. They must be made and then defended. Supine leaders of institutions and political activists should be careful what they wish for. If we do deconstruct the West, who or what will replace it?

# 1

# Identity politics, decolonisation and social theory

To understand the prevalence of identity politics in Britain, it is necessary to unpack some of the key ideas and theories that have underpinned its rise. These have arisen within Left social theory and incubated within the university system. This chapter examines the theories and ideas the decolonisation movement draws on. We begin by looking at the ways in which Left social theory attached itself onto revolutionary movements in the global South.

## Race and revolution

The ideologically coded reading of the history of the West and the non-Western world has long been part of the historical worldview of left-wing critical theorists. In the immediate post-war period, and in the context of European colonial dissolution, the Soviet Union and the Left more generally supported anti-colonial movements, including the non-aligned movement. In January 1961, Soviet premier Nikita Khrushchev pledged support for 'wars of national liberation' throughout the world. Throughout the 1960s, 'Third-Worldism' emerged, largely due to the failure of radical socialist ideas to inspire the desired revolutionary tumult among the Western working class. It fused a form of revolutionary Marxism with a critique of racism and revolution, with many left-wing intellectuals transferring their hopes of social change to the developing world.

At the time, the global South was undergoing a process of decolonisation. The costs and tumult of the Second World War meant the principal European colonial powers of France and Britain could no longer hold onto their colonies. In some cases, this was a smooth process of transition and, in many others, it was often bloody and violent. For example, the war in Vietnam started when the French attempted to thwart the nationalist forces of the Viet Cong, and France's failure to suppress the insurgency gradually sucked the US in, as it attempted to prevent a domino effect of communist states across Asia.

These anti-colonial and often nationalist insurgencies in Africa, Asia and Latin America were seized upon by left-wing social theorists as beacons of hope and liberation against centuries of Western domination and capitalism. They would, the theorists argued, point the way towards a new emancipated future for humankind, and offered a degree of theoretical respite, given the failure of revolutionary ideas to take hold in the major capitalist economies.

The Chinese communist theorist, Lin Biao, captured the sentiment well in 1965:

> the proletarian revolutionary movement has for various reasons been temporarily held back in the North American and west European capitalist countries, while the people's revolutionary movement in Asia, Africa, and Latin America has been growing vigorously . . . In the final analysis, the whole cause of world revolution hinges on the revolutionary struggles of the Asian, African, and Latin American peoples who make up the overwhelming majority of the world's population. The socialist countries should regard it as their internationalist duty to

support the people's revolutionary struggles in Asia, Africa, and Latin America.[1]

Arguably one of the most important theorists was Frantz Fanon, whose hugely influential book, *The Wretched of the Earth*, was published in 1961. It was one of the first major works to draw out the intersection between a politics antithetical to the West, forms of racial identity politics and their instrumental capacity to act as a means of widespread political mobilisation for revolutionary change.

For Fanon, the Third World anti-colonial movements were challenging imperialism and a form of international hierarchy organised along racial lines. Violence against Europeans was a form of self-realisation for the revolutionary movements of the global South. To 'shoot down a European is to kill two birds with one stone', Jean Paul-Sartre argued in his Foreword to Fanon's book. By doing so, it is possible to 'destroy an oppressor and the man he oppresses at the same time: there remain a dead man, and a free man'.[2]

The moral impetus for this programme of Western deconstruction comes from a view of history that argues that the West's economic hegemony emerged from the exploitation of the Third World. Dependency theory argues that a core of wealthy, capitalist and former colonial states have attained economic primacy by exploiting the resources of what dependency theorists argued is the periphery, or the Third World. Western colonialism, its history of slavery, and what is alleged to be post-colonial exploitation is explained by the integration of this periphery within the global economy that is controlled by the core capitalist powers.[3] Building on these insights, the Marxist theoretician Immanuel Wallerstein's world-systems analysis argued that capitalism arose in the core through a crisis of feudalism that transformed the relations of production and essentially gave Europe an early head start on the road to industrialisation.[4] This new 'world system', while dynamic in terms of potential shifts in economic power, served to create an advantage for Europe over the underdeveloped Third World and continues to explain inequality today.

Many decolonial theorists draw upon these ideas in their view of the UK and in order to give a moral impetus to their critique. The UK's pre-eminence did not emerge from its science and the advent of the Industrial Revolution. Instead, 'we need to trace how genocide, slavery and colonialism are the key foundation stones upon which the West was built', argues Kehinde Andrews, one of the UK's leading critical race theorists. Echoing the rejection of the Enlightenment tradition, he continues that its legacy 'was essential in providing the intellectual basis for Western imperialism, justifying white supremacy through scientific rationality'.[5]

Given this worldview, Great Britain's status and history are thus said to be built on a fundamentally immoral foundation. This view of history provides the impetus for the decolonial critique of British history, its institutions and, more broadly, the moral repudiation and challenge to Western civilisation itself. When a global perspective on the development of capitalism is applied, 'we develop a new appreciation of the centrality of slavery, in the US and elsewhere, in the emergence of modern capitalism', argues Sven Beckert, one of the leading proponents of what is called the New History of Capitalism thesis. This thesis maintains that slavery was central to the West's economic development. He continues that 'industrial capitalism and the Great Divergence' between the West and the developing world, 'in fact emerged from the violent cauldron of slavery, colonialism, and the expropriation of land'.[6]

However, despite the hopes of Western radicals, many of the post-colonial states that drew their inspiration from Marxism and Maoism did not turn into utopias based on human equality. Instead, most morphed into highly oppressive dictatorships. Mao's cultural revolution alone accounted for 45 million deaths.[7] As Marxism fell out of fashion in Western universities, coupled with the collapse of the Soviet Union in 1991, many radical intellectuals began to look elsewhere to help explain what they saw as the continued domination between the West and the global South and inequality within the West itself.

Many commentators, especially those of the centre-Right, view identity politics as a modern form of Marxism.[8] Modern identity politics do indeed share a common critique of Western civilisation and a political project of its deconstruction. However, modern identity politics emerge mainly from French poststructuralism and not Marxism.

The 1930s Marxism of Antonio Gramsci and the Frankfurt School was driven by a central puzzle: how can we explain the fact that socialist ideas have not led to the widespread transformation of Western societies. This puzzle took on added salience given the fact that according to Marxist theory, western European capitalist societies had deep class contradictions and, according to the dialectal theory of history, should see their revolutionary transformation into socialism.

In answer to this puzzle, and rather than address the many flaws of Marxism, Gramsci and the Frankfurt school argued that this lack of class consciousness among the working class could be explained by the role of culture and ideas. The 'power of corporate capitalism has stifled the emergence' of a revolutionary 'consciousness and imagination; its mass media have adjusted the rational and emotional faculties to its market and its policies and steered them to defense of its dominion', argued Herbert Marcuse, one of cultural Marxism's leading theorists. However, where 'capitalist culture has not yet reached into every house or hut, the system of stabilizing needs has its limits'. This is especially the case among what he terms the 'ghetto population and the unemployed in the United States; this is also the case of the laboring classes in the more backward capitalist countries'.[9] In this, there was an explicit fusion between race, revolution and culture. 'Class conflicts are being superseded or blotted out by race conflicts: color lines become economic and political realities – a development rooted in the dynamic of late imperialism and its struggle for new methods of internal and external colonization.'[10]

In short, the argument was that the working class was in effect brainwashed by various ideologies, including religion (the opiate of the masses) or nationalism, which pitted the working class in one nation against those of another. In later developments in Marxist social theory, the Marxist intellectual Louis Althusser, prominent in 1950s France, even went so far as to invent a theory of 'ideological state apparatuses' that he argued frame the ways of interpreting the world in a way that reinforces the power of the capitalist ruling class and economic system.[11]

French poststructuralism drew upon these ideas on the centrality of culture and ideas, but rejected the materialism, political economy and role that social classes play in political transformation.[12] We see this carrying over in many left-wing parties today; those that have moved away from social class to one of identity and issues beyond class such as environmentalism. In that sense, the poststructuralists and their modern identity politics descendants are as hostile to the philosophical underpinnings of Marxism as they are to what they tend to characterise as an inherently oppressive Western civilisation. Marxism was ultimately a teleological view of history, which saw it unfolding towards a communist utopia, and driven in turn by the contradictions in capitalism.

These new critical social theories moved away from a class-based analysis of capitalism. Instead, they argued for the centrality of culture and ideas in helping explain the social relations of the Western world. In moving away from a materialist account of history, rooted in objective relations of production that gave rise to antagonistic social classes, priority was now placed on sets of theories grounded in subjectivity, emotion and ideas as being the motors of oppression but also possible social change.[13] These new post-Marxist critical thinkers argued that if you want to effect radical social change you must change the way people understand the world. In this, they asserted a social constructivist theory of knowledge: the world does not present itself to us unmediated. Rather the social ideas we hold actively shape the world itself.

These ideas were expounded most forcefully in the postmodernist movement that began and then spread beyond its native France in the 1960s. Today, it dominates in the social sciences and humanities in US and UK universities. Its chief theorists were Michel Foucault and Jacques Derrida, whose ideas are crucial to understand today's decolonisation movement and the power of identity politics more generally.

## Post-Marxist social theory and decolonisation

Michel Foucault is arguably one of the most influential thinkers of the twentieth century. He was the Professor of History of Systems of Thought at France's elite Collège de France. Moving beyond the materialism of Marxism, Foucault, like other postmodernists, instead argued for the importance of ideas in shaping human societies and cultures. He also shared the left-wing romanticism with Third World revolutionary movements. For example, although an openly gay man, he eulogised the 1979 Islamist revolution in Iran, and saw it as radically transgressive of Western forms of rationality and the binary logic of modernity.[14]

Postmodernists are primarily interested in a branch of philosophy called epistemology, which is concerned with knowledge and how we know what we know. Postmodernists adopt a social constructivist epistemology. For them, meaning and truth cannot be found outside of human perception itself and everything is thus in the eye of the beholder.

To give an illustrative example: as we drive around in a car, we understand the rules around traffic lights. However, there is nothing natural or objective to this system of meaning insofar as they rely on intersubjectively shared understandings of the inherent rules (or grammar) around roads and the control of traffic. There is no objectively true reason why a red traffic light means we stop, and a green light means we go. When we see a red light, it is our shared ideas and cultural 'scripts' that mean we stop or go – not the alleged objectively 'real' nature of the colour red or green. As such, for postmodernists, social meaning is constructed from these shared ideas and meanings and not from the 'referent' to which those ideas refer and that is outside human consciousness (in this case the physical traffic light).

Foucault took these ideas and added another layer. He argued that our shared ideas (what he called 'discourses' or 'epistemes') are not innocent but are intimately bound up with power relations. In mapping this relationship between power and knowledge, he invented a 'genealogical' method to trace how these shared and common understandings have changed over time and throughout history, and how these have shaped power relations in society.

For example, he was interested in the history of madness and traced how dominant understandings of mental illness have changed in Europe. In the Renaissance period, those classified as 'insane' were often portrayed as possessing a deeper form of wisdom and truth and access to the unknown world and were often celebrated in art and literature. As the Age of Reason began in the seventeenth century, Foucault argued that the discourse (shared meanings and power relations) of madness changed, with the medicalisation and classification of those as mentally ill as needing confinement. The 'unreason' of madness was a destabilising threat to 'reason' and thus needed to be confined, often in huge institutions and on the margins of society.

As such, while the biological reality of mental illness remained the same, the discourse through which it was understood changed radically – from tolerance to one of confinement. Foucault's insight was that this change in discourse thus meant how society treated the mentally ill underwent a profound shift that had implications for power relations between those classified as insane and those not. In short, as our understandings change and thus classifications, so does the way society treat those things that are being classified.

In this, Foucault flatly rejected the notion of objectivity or truth like many other postmodern thinkers. For Foucault, there is no such thing as one truth or scientific standard, but many ways of understanding the world, all of which have their own implicit biases, knowledge claims and power relations. As he argued, 'in any given culture and at any given moment, there is always only one episteme that defines the conditions of possibility of all knowledge, whether expressed in a theory or silently invested in a practice'.[15] His work sought to question and challenge these dominant 'epistemes'. As such, and like other postmodern thinkers, Foucault endorsed a form of judgemental relativism whereby any kind of standard or indeed objective measure should be abandoned in favour of situating one's own ideas or emotions within specific cultural biases.

Developing these ideas, the French postmodern philosopher Jacques Derrida also sought to challenge the notion of objectivity and truth within Western philosophy and placed primacy on culture and ideas. Derrida championed a 'deconstructive' philosophical method that sought to decentre the search for a metaphysical truth and meaning that he argued was central to Western philosophy. His ideas have helped profoundly to shape identity politics and to 'decolonise' movement in the UK.

For Derrida, Western philosophy sought meaning primarily through the arbitrary construction and imposition of hierarchically organised binaries that privileged one of the pairs over and above the other. He argued that these binary structures organise human experience and are maintained through exclusionary acts. In creating something, something else will always get left out; what is called 'othering' within postmodern theory.

Derrida argued that these binaries serve to repress and entrench hierarchies on a cultural level. Examples would include mind over body, male over female, civilised over primitive, etc. These binaries are alleged to have helped structure our knowledge of the world and, in keeping with social constructivism, they ultimately shape its very existence.

Like Foucault, Derrida argued for a form of moral relativism with the goal of the deconstructive method being the exposure and 'denaturalisation' of our taken-for-granted assumptions and ways of seeing the world. He sought to show that all knowledge is contingent and arbitrary.

There was an implicit politically playful element to the postmodernist movement. Its social constructivism sought to question and deconstruct the Enlightenment quest for truth, objectivity and the discovery of a world 'out there'. The confidence of Western civilisation, itself said to be bound up with its self-image of rationality and the scientific method, was to be undermined by exposing the frailty of all truth claims.

## Post-colonialism

This link between postmodern theories and the critique of Western colonialism found its apogee in the work of the post-colonial theorists. Many post-colonial ideas underpin the decolonise movement and identity politics more broadly. Post-colonialism draws on postmodern theories but is more explicitly politically activist and geared towards social and political transformation.

As Hutcheon argues, while the links between these two related bodies of theory are clear, post-colonial theory 'possesses a strong political motivation that is intrinsic to its oppositionality', while postmodernism 'is politically ambivalent' as it exists within and is complicit with 'the cultural dominants within which it inescapably exists'. Post-colonialism seeks to move beyond the 'postmodern limits of deconstructing existing orthodoxies into the realms of social and political action'.[16]

The lead post-colonial theorist was Edward Said, who applied postmodern ideas to the colonial relationship between the West and the global South, especially the Arab world. His work emphasises the allegedly 'Orientalist' nature of Western knowledge of the Arab Orient. He argues that this Orientalist discourse helped shape Western perceptions of the non-Western world. 'My contention', he says, is that 'without examining Orientalism as a discourse one cannot possibly understand the enormously systematic discipline by which European culture was able to manage – and even produce – the Orient politically, sociologically, ideologically, scientifically, and imaginatively during the post-Enlightenment period.'[17]

Drawing on Derrida's theory of binaries and deconstruction, combined with Foucault's theory of knowledge and power, Said argued that while Western Orientalism portrayed the West as rational and sophisticated, the Arab world was seen as irrational, backward and exotic. Moreover, Western Orientalism was inherently Eurocentric insofar as it emphasised European values at the expense of the 'other'. Said linked his postmodern critique of knowledge and power relations with the wider politics of European colonisation and subsequent decolonisation of the Middle East. The key assertion is not just that our dominant ways of seeing the world and orientalist discourses are racist as far as they privilege a European worldview but, using Foucault's ideas, help to produce the non-Western world that can then be acted upon by Western colonisers.

As such, history as we know it 'became the product of the West in its actions upon others', argues Bhambra. Moreover,

it 'naturalised and justified the West's material domination of the "other" and in this way suggested the complicity
between Orientalism as scholarly discourse and as imperial
institution'.[18] In the words of Olivia U. Rutazibwa and Robbie
Shilliam, 'the Eurocentric conception of the modern world,
the projection of the other as inferior, dangerous, less capable
or "not there yet" is naturalised conceptually and narratively'.
Importantly, although we now live in a post-colonial era, colonial discourses continue to naturalise dominant ways of seeing
and thus structuring the world. It is this 'naturalisation that
makes global politics quintessentially post-colonial politics'.[19]

In this way, post-colonial theorists argue that Western colonialism not only has legacy effects in terms of politics and
economic justice, but ongoing cultural effects too. Drawing on
postmodern and post-colonial theory, these implicit power/
knowledge relations are said to continue to resonate within
the domestic politics of former colonial societies themselves
and structure the way these societies view non-European
minorities both domestically and internationally. As Aníbal
Quijano argues, 'Europe's hegemony over the new model of
global power concentrated all forms of the control of subjectivity, culture, and especially knowledge and the production of
knowledge under its hegemony.'[20]

## Decolonisation theory and British universities

There is a very strong political bias on campuses. 76% of
academics in the social sciences in the world's leading universities self-identify as left wing with 16% identifying as
'far Left'.[21] Just one in ten are on the Right. Given the role
that British universities have historically played in educating
elites, coupled with the informal ideological hegemony that
progressives have within the humanities and social sciences
faculties in the UK, it is perhaps unsurprising that the British

university system has become a key focus for the decolonising movement. Universities are also responsible for educating cultural elites, and thus are a major source of helping push progressive 'social justice', justified as necessary because of their alleged historical sins. Choat captures this logic succinctly: the 'university in particular is an important focus of decolonisation because European – and especially British – universities have historically been deeply imbricated in the colonial project'.[22]

In their seminal book, *Decolonising the University*, Gurminder K. Bhambra, Dalia Gebrial and Kerem Nişancıoğlu argue that given the history of European colonialism 'it becomes difficult to turn away from the Western university as a key site through which colonialism – and colonial knowledge in particular – is produced, consecrated, institutionalised and naturalised'. Importantly, the colonial discourse is said to be still deeply embedded within UK universities today and the fall of 'formal empires did little to change the logic of Western universities'. Indeed, the very existence of political activists calling for a decolonised curriculum apparently proves that 'the content of university knowledge remains principally governed by the West for the West'.[23]

Similarly, Shilliam claims that any pushback or critique of the decolonisation agenda is a form of political racial conspiracy. When critiquing his ideas and those of other post-colonial theorists, he argues that there is 'something of a far more heinous nature going on', whereby the 'political class look upon the changes to Britain's (and the West's) population pyramid with trepidation'. In response to the 'base of the pyramid growing relentlessly blacker, browner, poorer' these political elites seek to 'preserve the whiteness of elite cultural reproduction in sites that are currently most detached from the pyramid's base'.[24] In essence, universities are alleged to be key vectors of racial privilege and white supremacy through the maintenance of hegemonic 'whiteness', with political elites who are directly responsible for the liberal immigration regime that prevails in the UK somehow seeing the results of their own policies with trepidation.

In invoking this concept of whiteness, Shilliam is drawing upon critical race theory and what has become a seemingly legitimate field of academic enquiry called 'whiteness studies'. It is important to unpack some of these ideas given their importance to the decolonisation critique of British institutions.

## The malign nature of 'whiteness'

In one of the defining papers on 'whiteness' Teresa Guess distinguishes between what she terms racism by intent and racism by consequence. The former approximates to the general understanding of racism and 'operates at the individual level and is manifested as racial prejudice and discrimination toward non-white individuals'.

Racism by consequence, however, is alleged to operate at a macro level and represents a move away from personalised racism to how racism becomes hardwired into social practices and institutions. Guess argues that as a 'result, racial prejudices may decline over time, yet more subtle patterns of discrimination persist, supported by the inertia of custom, bureaucratic procedure, impersonal routine, and even law'.[25]

This is an important distinction, because as we saw in the introduction, racism and discrimination has significantly diminished in the UK since the advent of mass immigration in the 1960s. A range of anti-discrimination laws, coupled with shifts in social attitudes means that the UK is a far more tolerant place than it was fifty years ago. However, Guess's distinction between intent and consequence means that although we have seen increasingly progressive attitudes in the UK's race relations, racial disparities in terms of consequence allegedly remain. That is, racism can be hardwired into institutions, take on a depersonalised form, and persist even as discriminatory attitudes decline: what is popularly known as 'systemic racism'.

What is the main indicator of this form of systemic 'racism by consequence'? Guess argues that the lead indicators are unequal outcomes between racial groups: 'differential educational opportunities, economic differentials between whites and non-whites, residential segregation, health care access, and death rate differentials between whites and non-whites'.[26] For Guess, the concept of 'whiteness' is thus not rooted in a biological foundation. Instead, and using the theories of social constructivism outlined above, whiteness is defined by social meanings. 'Uncovering or deconstructing the social construction of "race" and whiteness begins with a definition of the situation or context in which these ideas tend to define social interaction patterns.'[27]

Whiteness is thus said to be a social discourse. To use postmodern phraseology, it helps structure a hierarchal binary between white and non-white groups that privileges the former, becomes naturalised and thus reproduces unequal outcomes between groups in institutionalised settings and contexts.[28] In short, 'all whites, by virtue of systemic white privilege that is inseparable from white ways of being, are implicated in the production and reproduction of systemic racial injustice'.[29]

In developing this idea of whiteness, the UK's leading critical race theorist, Kehinde Andrews, has applied it at great length to the history of race relations in the UK. For Andrews, 'whiteness' is hardwired throughout British society, and is, in his view, a form of mental illness. It 'induces a form of psychosis framed by its irrationality, which is beyond any rational engagement'. Moreover, and perhaps more worrying, white people use whiteness to cope with 'the reality that Western capitalism is built on and maintained by racial exploitation'. Despite whiteness being irrational, he maintains it remains a useful way to guilt-trip and ultimately make white people responsible for solving alleged racial disparities within the UK. 'Whiteness' helps focus 'attention on how a broader racist culture shapes white people's identities, and brings to the fore the responsibilities that white people have for addressing racism.' Echoing the earlier ideas of post-colonial theorists such as Frantz Fanon, Andrews continues that by 'forcing white people to confront their complicity in the system, the aim is to make them reborn as allies to the dark oppressed peoples of the world'.[30] This is allegedly necessary, according to one of America's leading critical race theorists, because white 'people raised in Western society are conditioned into a white supremacist worldview because it is the bedrock of our society and its institutions . . . Entering the conversation with this understanding is freeing because it allows us to focus on how – rather than if – our racism is manifest.'[31]

In this way, we can begin to see the contours of the decolonial critique of the West and its institutions, especially universities that are seen as deeply complicit with colonial discourses and evidenced through alleged entrenched whiteness and unequal outcomes.

## Summary

What are the key points we can take away from the above? First, postmodern theories emerged from a deeper critique of Marxism and the failure of left-wing ideas to inspire the working classes in western Europe. Instead, an emphasis was placed on the role that culture and ideology play in shaping perceptions. Theorists such as Foucault, Derrida and Said developed a body of theory that looked at the ways discourse and power has operated within the West and how these discourses have suffused with how we understand the non-Western world. The key political goal has been to 'decentre' truth and science and deconstruct Western civilisation. The certainty that comes from having 'the truth' is seen as being largely responsible for asserting the supremacy of Western epistemologies and ways of knowing over the marginalised and oppressed.

Second, identity politics and the decolonial critique draws its moral power from a view of history that conflates Western colonialism and slavery. This view states that the West enjoys its standard of living not because of its science, institutions or the Industrial Revolution, but by theft on a global scale, backed up by a form of racialised imperial violence. This history of colonialism continues to explain the wealth gap between the West and the global South and there is a moral duty for today's radical intellectuals to highlight this history in order to help drive social justice in the world today and call for restitution.

Third, and building on these ideas, the decolonisation movement in the UK seeks to deconstruct dominant colonial discourse, ways of being and the structural privileges said to be inherent to 'whiteness' and Western civilisation. Given the importance of the university system, the decolonial critique is part of a broader political campaign to promote 'social justice'. This critique is more than simply diversifying academic sources on courses but extends to challenging the very foundations of the British university system itself. 'Whiteness' is a structural manifestation of these entrenched privileges that is said to reproduce unequal outcomes for ethnic minorities. The decolonial critique rejects objectivity and science, and their wellspring within the Western Enlightenment. Rather than reason being universal and helping drive progress, the Enlightenment, its values, and the institutions it helped inculcate are tarnished with the suffering of the developing world. The apogee of this suffering was the transatlantic slave trade and the role that Britain played in its development. From this historical role, decolonial theorists argue that a racial legacy has been hardwired into British institutions with forms of whiteness and white privilege throughout British institutions and UK universities. It is the job of white people to become aware of this, and act as enabling allies in a broader form of a new 'anti-racism', which views white people as collectively guilty because of 'whiteness', that is itself a form of psychosis and mental illness.

As Maldonado-Torres et al. argue, 'philosophy as a field or a discipline in modern Western universities remains a bastion of Eurocentrism, whiteness in general, and white heteronormative male structural privilege and superiority in particular'. They continue that the curriculum reflects this skew with an 'overwhelming absence of people of colour in classrooms and philosophical reading lists'. This is a situation that is 'part of the legacy of Western imperialism, racialised slavery, white heteronormative male supremacy, and segregation, which highly elevated the value of civilisation and abstract universality, and exclusively linked them with concepts, norms and values that were considered to be of European provenance'.[32]

To decolonise, then, is a moral and political call to action that involves more than simply diversifying reading lists within British universities. As Akel argues, the decolonising of education 'should not be mistaken for "diversification", as diversity can still exist within this Western bias. Decolonisation goes further and deeper in challenging the institutional hierarchy and monopoly on knowledge, moving out of a Western framework.' She continues that 'it is impossible to divorce our worldview – including our political and moral values – from the subject matter we're taught. If we don't challenge the colonial roots of our education, we are ultimately breathing life into an ideological framework born out of an Empire steeped in blood. The task then, is for each of us consciously and intently to work to decolonise both our minds and the institutions that uphold this.' In so doing, decolonisation activists can transform Western societies in radical ways. 'There are revolutionary futures that we can imagine for ourselves through alternative ways of understanding the world that do not start, end and seek validation from darkness.'[33]

This chapter has unpacked and examined the broad range of theories that underline the decolonial critique of British institutions. It did so to provide the reader with a deeper understanding of key ideas and themes. In the next chapter, we will examine how these ideas have been adopted almost wholesale by British universities and pushed as a new orthodoxy to restructure our centres of learning and the worldview of our educated younger generation.

# 2

# Racism on campus

The previous chapter examined the theories underlying the decolonisation movement and identity politics. This chapter moves from these more abstract theories to examine how these have been applied in British universities. Across the Anglophone West, especially in the US and the UK, the shocking killing of George Floyd in America in 2020 and the rise of the Black Lives Matter movement placed the issue of race and racism centre stage. In response, many universities have committed to decolonisation and the associated ideas of critical race theory (CRT) and the CRT-inspired theories of 'whiteness'.

This chapter shows how this has played out across the UK university sector. I am especially interested in teasing out the key arguments and data that justify the decolonisation agenda.

## The EHRC and racism in British universities

As we have seen, the decolonisation agenda in British universities is driven by a specific set of claims as to the widespread and allegedly systemically racist nature of the British university system.

The Equality and Human Rights Commission (EHRC) is the UK's leading independent statutory body responsible for encouraging equality and diversity. In October 2019, it released a series of shocking reports that purported to show that racism is endemic in Britain's higher education sector. The EHRC's claims were picked up by media outlets worldwide and triggered a wave of responses among the sector's leaders. The reports argued that the problem was so significant that new laws and regulations were needed to address it adequately.

Following the EHRC's reports, its then Chief Executive, Rebecca Hilsenrath, argued that universities were 'not only out of touch with the extent that [racism] is occurring on their campuses, some are also completely oblivious to the issue'.[1] Professor Julia Buckingham, then president of universities UK, representing 140 British universities, described the findings as 'sad and shocking' and called on vice-chancellors to make tackling racism across the UK university a top priority.[2] Nicola Dandridge, then chief executive of the Office for Students – the independent regulator of higher education in England – described the EHRC's findings as 'deeply troubling'. Jo Grady, general secretary of the University and College Union (UCU), the UK's most prominent academic trade union, said: 'Universities should be safe spaces for all staff and students, free from harassment and discrimination, but this report shows there is still much work to be done to make this a reality.'[3] Then universities minister Chris Skidmore, a Conservative Member of Parliament, called on all senior administrators to prioritise 'a zero-tolerance culture' regarding all types of harassment and said it was 'simply not good enough' that some senior leaders were not tackling the issue. Ms Grady said the 'minister is right to call for a zero-tolerance approach to all harassment and hate crime, but he must be ready to back this up with sanctions where the sector fails to act'.[4]

The report showed that in the academic year 2018/19, 92 of the 1,009 white and ethnic minority students surveyed, 8% had experienced racial harassment.[5] Extrapolating from these figures, the *Guardian* reported that 'A third of those said they reported racist incidents to their university, the equivalent of 60,000 students nationwide.'[6]

The EHRC also released another report: 'Tackling racial harassment: Universities challenged'.[7] This report was based on an inquiry targeted at 'people with direct experience of being racially harassed and those who had witnessed racial harassment taking place or supported a victim of it'. It was designed to gather evidence from a three-and-a-half-year period between the 2015/16 academic year and January 2019. The inquiry gathered evidence and closed in February 2019. It found that:

> Universities received an average of just 2.3 total staff complaints of racial harassment and 3.6 total student complaints of racial harassment between the start of the 2015/16 academic year and January 2019. Around four in ten institutions in our university survey (38%) reported having received no complaints of racial harassment from staff; around three in ten (29%) received no reports from students. Almost one in five institutions (18%) received no complaints of racial harassment from either group.[8]

Despite this, Universities UK (UUK), the UK's preeminent body for university vice-chancellors, released their framework for action to help challenge this alleged epidemic of racism across British campuses. Its November 2020 report, called *Tackling Racial Harassment in Higher Education*, sent a powerful and unmistakable message to university vice chancellors that hard-wired the decolonisation agenda into British universities.[9]

## UUK: Leading anti-racist cultural change

The Chair of UUK's Advisory Group on tackling racial harassment in higher education, Professor David Richardson, outlined a bold call for change across the university sector. Arguing that personal transformation or change at a single university is simply not good enough, he argued that we 'must acknowledge the institutional racism and systemic issues that pervade the entire higher education sector, in all institutions, if we are to bring about meaningful change'. He continued that to this end, the UUK's new guidance will help support 'universities in delivering long-term change in institutional culture and behaviours' while encouraging 'institutional leaders to turn words into tangible measures that bring about sustainable cultural change'. In so doing, society will benefit, as universities will 'shape the minds and attitudes of the next generation'.[10]

Contrary to the popular perception of universities as beacons of progressive change and social justice, the UUK report warns that the alleged racism 'endemic in UK society . . . also pervades higher education'. Its key recommendations include improving 'awareness and understanding of racism, racial harassment, white privilege and microaggressions among all staff and students, including through anti-racist training'. In helping this process of mentally reprogramming students and staff, the UUK guidance explicitly adopts a decolonising framework. Drawing on the theories we examined in the previous chapter, the report argued that this will help as the UK is a country characterised by 'white domination' that 'is normalised and therefore seen as natural' and that benefits 'white people, who as a collective group benefit from structural racism overall'.[11]

Writing on WonkHE, a leading UK higher education website, Professor Richardson argued that when 'embarking on changing institutional culture, the first step must be to acknowledge the existence of structural racism in our institutions'. He then foregrounded the importance of people's own experiences, emotions and anecdotes, to fully understand 'the lived experience of staff and students and make an effort to understand concepts such as white privilege, allyship, and microaggressions'.[12] WonkHE's editor outlined the disconnect between the perception of universities 'as liberal, tolerant spaces, to acknowledge the ways that systems and cultures can produce inequitable outcomes'. She continued to outline the collective racial guilt of white people, all of whom benefit from universities 'because white people have consistently failed to challenge or dismantle the structures that tend to benefit us, we are all de facto complicit in that process without having to be aggressively racist in our attitudes or behaviours'.[13]

How to counter white domination and help shape the next generation's minds? The UUK makes several suggestions, including the need for university leaders to implement new systems to monitor and deal with the prevalence of racial 'microaggressions' and ingrained and systemic 'white privilege'. In terms of teaching, university curricula need to be fully decolonised as what is currently taught, as well as the dominance of white scholars on reading lists, merely help 'perpetuate existing inequalities and are unlikely to reflect the experience or viewpoints of many members of the student and staff body'.[14]

To help with this transformation process, the UUK report calls on young undergraduates to audit their professors' courses to ensure diverse representation within materials used in lectures and tutorials. In training staff, universities should 'incorporate the concepts of white privilege and white fragility, white allyship, microaggressions and intersectionality, as well as racialised unconscious bias training'. In this way, an 'inclusive culture and environment' will be created 'by setting the tone and expectations of student and staff behaviour'. In so doing, senior university managers will inaugurate a truly 'anti-racist' university and are asked to 'commit' to making sure that there will be 'consequences' when this drive for inclusivity is in any way 'breached'.[15]

## The Race Equality Charter

In the mission to create a more inclusive and equitable university system by expunging white domination, many institutions have adopted the 'Race Equality Charter' (REC). The Charter has been developed by an organisation called Advance HE, a multimillion-pound publicly funded body that plays the role of a 'single sector agency for equality and diversity, learning and teaching, and leadership and governance in higher education'. Advance HE currently provides professional development programmes and events, fellowships and professional recognition, with more than 140,000 teaching and learning fellows across the UK.[16]

The REC's foundational principle is that 'racial inequalities are a significant issue within higher education'. Its charter 'provides a framework through which institutions work to identify and self-reflect on institutional and cultural barriers standing in the way of minority ethnic staff and students'.[17]

Its REC seeks to drive through cultural change in universities through accreditation, whereby universities submit themselves for assessment to the REC whose assessors may award bronze or silver stars for attainment in crucial areas, including diversity of staff, promotion of BAME[18] academics to senior roles, successfully decolonising curricula and teaching and, more generally, raising awareness of structural racism and 'whiteness' on UK campuses. Award holders must submit their reports showing that constant changes are being made to retain their award. If they fail to make adequate changes, they must resubmit with additional evidence within a grace period or they will be stripped of their recognition.

Unsurprisingly, there are strong intellectual synergies between the decolonise movement and the REC. A survey of the university sector commissioned by Advance HE in preparation for its REC was aimed at those running the Equality, Diversity and Inclusion committees in universities. These committees are becoming increasingly influential within university bureaucracies. They exist to police the implementation of the REC and other social justice-accredited charters such as the gender audit, Athena SWAN.

Advance HE's survey asked respondents to comment on the statement 'Our institution wants to decolonise the curriculum, teaching and learning' and records that 94.1% of those involved ranked this as 'moderately important', 'very or extremely important'. Of those, 29.4% described it as 'extremely important'.[19] The same questionnaire also asks 'What steps are you taking to prepare your institution for becoming a REC member?' where one of the check boxes is labelled 'Starting/continuing decolonising the curriculum and teaching and learning'. The report shows that 63.2% of respondents checked this box.[20]

Advance HE's REC has become the key means of cultural transformation of UK universities through incentivised accreditation and enforcement by newly empowered EDI bureaucracies across the UK higher education sector. Like the EHRC and the UUK reports, the REC highlights critical areas that need to be addressed in helping to eliminate alleged systemic racism. These include the degree attainment gap, decolonising the curriculum and microaggressions. We will now consider each of these in turn and the essential claims.

## The degree attainment gap

One key indicator of alleged racial discrimination in the UK higher education sector is a degree attainment gap between students of different ethnicities. A major 2019 UUK report called *Black, Asian and Minority Ethnic Student Attainment at UK Universities, #Closingthegap* argued that students' race and ethnicity can significantly affect their degree outcomes. It stated that 'the gap between the likelihood of White students and students from black, Asian or minority ethnic (BAME) backgrounds getting a first- or upper-second-class degree is among the most stark – 13% among 2017–18 graduates'.[21]

Former Director of the School of Oriental and African Studies (SOAS), Baroness Amos, stated that universities would be failing 'a generation of students if we don't act now to reduce the BAME (black and minority ethnic) attainment gap . . . Universities must act and are transparent in their approach so black, Asian and minority ethnic students are given the best chance of success. Inaction is not an option. Universities should be places where opportunity and aspiration come together.'[22] Amatey Doku, then Vice President of the National Union of Students, argued that 'universities have presided over significant gaps in attainment between BME students and white students for far too long' and called on 'all senior leaders in the higher education sector' to take 'proactive steps . . . to eradicate these unjust gaps in attainment once and for all'. This gap is assumed to be part of a broader pattern of structural injustice and inequality linked to race. Universities UK has argued that the ethnic minority attainment gap 'does not exist in isolation within higher education, but is part of the wider structural nature of racial inequality in the UK'.[23]

Drawing from the critical race theory that we examined in the last chapter, the report distinguishes between personal and systemic forms of discrimination and erases all human agency or responsibility. Instead, the report argues that the attainment gap is not down to 'skills, knowledge or experience' but is instead explained by 'societal or institutional structures and the discrimination that exists within them' and as such, the 'responsibility for the inequalities in attainment' are to be 'placed with the institution' and not students themselves.

Beyond this systemic and institutional argument to help explain disparities between students of different ethnicities, the report also claims that a lack of role models for BAME students is a key factor. Depressingly, the report argues BAME academics that work within UK universities can 'become overburdened with the responsibility of acting as role models and mentors, and this can also create a perception that the responsibility for addressing the attainment gap and related issues does not fall to other members of staff'.[24]

Across the UK, universities have responded to this attainment gap. 'The Black Lives Matter movement has been the impetus for us to do more to widen access', says David Gavaghan, chair of Oxford's graduate access working group. 'There is a strong overlap between socio-economic background and ethnicity.' To this end, Oxford has started the Black Academic Futures programme that provided up to ten new scholarships to black UK research students beginning studies at Oxford in 2021.[25] Former Sussex University Vice Chancellor Adam Tickell and Provost Saul Becker argued that 'we have to recognise uncomfortable truths in our own university', promising that the university leadership would start the work of 'identifying and challenging the structural, cultural and other barriers, practices and discourses to achieving racial justice and equality within our institution'.[26] This is a move welcomed by Daniel Akinbosede as Sussex 'is far from alone in only just beginning its journey to close the attainment gap . . . While student collaboration is definitely important, universities must look in the mirror and address the perpetuation of whiteness as normality.'[27] Goldsmiths University established its 'Racial Justice Goldsmiths staff team' in 2019, who are collectively 'working to advance racial justice; in their wide portfolio of work closing the degree awarding gap is a key priority'. The story is similar across the entire university sector.[28]

Beyond these initiatives, the National Union of Students' campaign 'Why Is My Curriculum White?' has focused on what is taught and by whom and its role in perpetuating alleged institutional racism. 'The White curriculum not only compromises the quality of education provided, it asserts irrational and unjust practices and has incredibly detrimental effects on both staff and students.' The NUS continues that, BME staff and students remain 'under-represented and under-stimulated by the content of their curricula, with their histories and ancestral narrative omitted from mainstream discourse. The White curriculum is also one of the major contributors to the BME attainment gap' and 'feeds into the feeling of isolation, marginalisation, alienation and exclusion'.[29]

In a 2022 follow-up report, the UUK noted areas of improvement in the attainment gap. From the 2019 figures, there are reduced awarding gaps in 2022 'across all ethnic groups, but the gap between white and black students has seen the most substantial reduction, from 23.5% to 18.4%'.[30] Nonetheless, there is still much more to do. The UUK recommends that all university board and committee meetings should 'include racial inequality as a standing item' and beyond the campus, 'Universities need to focus as much on the culture outside the classroom as the culture inside it' to 'connect with the lived experiences of BAME students'. In connecting with the lived experiences of BAME, university leaders should allow BAME students to reverse mentor 'senior leaders and managers', create more 'paid ambassador schemes for BAME students' and make sure 'accommodation, catering services and social events factor in the needs of diverse groups'. The report notes that universities are also introducing targeted fee reductions, employability initiatives throughout the curriculum and mentor schemes for BAME students.[31]

## Changing the curriculum

Building on the NUS campaign, the UUK has reinforced the need to decolonise the curriculum across the UK higher education sector. A lack of 'BAME-specific content' and a '"mainstream" way of thinking' they argue, has led to a form of brainwashing of BAME students, whereby they learn 'different attitudes, values and perspectives through the university environment' that 'typically reinforces social norms'.[32] Given this, more consideration should be 'given to understanding the effect that existing curriculums and content (and wider teaching and learning practices including assessment and feedback) might be having on student inclusivity, including where the social and cultural capital accrued by particular groups of students might be disproportionately valued'.

To address this alleged disproportionate value between BAME and white students, 'greater understanding and recognition of white privilege is needed in the UK'. including unconscious bias training, now being 'being piloted for many members of staff at universities' who, the UUK argue, should 'formally provide evidence of how they mitigate their biases on an ongoing basis' such as 'employees evidencing their commitment to equality, diversity and inclusion'.

The decolonisation of the curriculum goes far beyond a mere reflection on sources and a plurality of perspectives and seeks to radically reform the UK higher education sector. Advance HE's REC further incentivises widespread educational and cultural change so that its directives become mandatory. As it states, in 'developing solutions to racial inequalities, it is important that they are aimed at achieving long-term institutional culture change' while 'avoiding a deficit model where solutions are aimed at changing the individual'.[33] The language of Advance HE's REC has been lifted and cut and pasted across nearly every UK university's mission statement in their mission to hold or win the bronze and silver stars awarded by the REC, as even a cursory google search shows.[34]

Keele University's Decolonise network has been a leader in the decolonisation process. Its network argues that this is not simply the 'token inclusion of the intellectual achievements of non-white cultures. Rather, it involves a paradigm shift from a culture of exclusion and denial to the making of space for other political philosophies and knowledge systems.' They continue that university teaching 'remains largely Eurocentric and continues to reinforce white and Western dominance and privilege'. Diversification of reading lists and thinkers, however, is simply not enough. Where 'the curriculum includes the intellectual work of people racialised as other-than-white, it can still operate as a white curriculum'. As such, decolonising 'means identifying ways in which the university structurally reproduces colonial hierarchies; confronting, challenging and rejecting the status quo; and reimagining them and putting alternatives into practice for the benefit of our academic integrity and our social viability'.[35]

Several institutions are now undergoing structural changes to repurpose teaching and learning in the name of social justice. For example, King's College London is one of the UK's leading universities. Former Principal, Ed Byrne, committed his institution to 'decolonise the curriculum and liberate education at King's'.[36] Baroness Amos, a vocal advocate for the movement and former Director of SOAS, captured the sentiment well. The movement is interested in 'who is on the reading lists, how much are you enabling a critique of different approaches to subjects, who is being recognised as being someone who can make a valuable contribution on this? That applies as much to science subjects as it does to arts and humanities subjects.'[37] Exeter University has committed to 'implementing an Education Strategy that puts success for all at its heart and prioritises widening access and participation, international students' wellbeing and decolonising the curriculum'. To that end, new courses in the social sciences faculty must show how they now 'move away' from a 'white, Eurocentric' curriculum as part of their approval process. In one of the UUK's flagship case studies from De Montfort University, decolonising the curriculum activists have 'contributed to relevant committees to ensure that the decolonising agenda is integral to decision-making and strategic planning across the institution'.[38]

Aside from moving away from a white, Eurocentric curriculum, many UK universities are also exploring what are called 'indigenous worldviews' to help to be more inclusive and diverse. In its 2019 innovating pedagogy report, the Open University argued that as part of the decolonising journey it would include 'indigenous knowledge and ways of learning' rather than 'the colonisers' perspective'. (Perhaps a degree on pre-Norman Anglo-Saxon civilisation?) Either way, this form of academic practice will enable 'students to explore themselves and their values and to define success on their own terms . . . to maintain their cultural integrity (their needs) while succeeding academically (educational needs)'.[39]

King's College is currently developing its 'indigenous-led' research and teaching effort as part of this broader effort to include indigenous perspectives alongside 'white, Eurocentric' views. The 'King's Indigenous initiative' aims to build research collaborations between UK academics and experts in indigenous knowledge, such as medicine and traditional healing. The initiative's Directors have argued that it sets out to 'develop innovative approaches to global challenges by exploring, testing and applying First Peoples-centred concepts and practices of research, exchange and teaching' and to 'build new, "decolonised", robust, nurturing and sustainable structures of pedagogy'.

Serena Masino, lecturer in International Development at the University of Westminster, said it was 'informed by the objective to decolonise at least part of the medical knowledge we rely on today'.[40] The University of Kent's Centre for

Indigenous and Settler Colonial Studies also aims to 'actively contribute to strategies at the University of Kent and in UK HE more broadly to decolonise curricula, with particular emphasis on pedagogical and methodological practice'. A mission necessary to 'disrupt the colonial structures of settler states' by 'centring of Indigenous voices and anti/decolonial activism' while unsettling 'the structures of colonial dominance and examining settler–Indigenous interrelations'.[41]

At the University of Leicester, reforms designed to decolonise the curriculum have seen the end of teaching English language and medieval literature.[42] They explain that the reality is that universities currently 'influence and shape what counts as "legitimate" knowledge' and this knowledge normalises and privileges 'White history, cultural values, norms, practices, perspectives, experiences, and voices. While at the same time, they marginalise other forms of knowing – albeit in varying ways.' This process is the 'beginning of a revolutionary process which seeks to create a Higher Education system that is fully and racially inclusive and fit for the 21st century'.[43]

The oldest staff-led Decolonise working group in Cambridge, 'Decolonise Sociology', states that faculty members should prepare 'an annual audit of reading lists and annual reports on progress with the Decolonise Sociology agenda'. Their stated goal is the full 'integration of authors from the global South across the curriculum, and not just inclusion of non-white, non-European scholars on the reading lists but prioritisation of their work in the required reading'. This will help standardise the 'use of whiteness as a concept, thus racialising white people – "and not just in race studies or whiteness studies but in everything"' – the Decolonise Sociology at Cambridge website usefully explains. As such, this will 'help draw more attention to the problem of the extreme whiteness of Cambridge and the curriculum, and more emphasis on disrupting the reproduction of whiteness'.[44] Perhaps channelling this theme, Cambridge University academic Priyamvada Gopal tweeted:

'I'll say it again. White Lives Don't Matter. As white lives.' She was promoted to a professorship soon afterwards.[45]

Similarly at Cambridge, the Decolonise Movement has demanded restructuring heritage collections and archives across the university. The Decolonise Archaeology and Decolonise History of Art and Architecture groups authored an open letter to the University of Cambridge Museums (UCM) demanding that collections be reorganised and relabelled after a 'UCM-wide colonial audit conducted by paid researchers', which would lead to indigenous artefacts being repatriated.[46] In response to a similar student letter, the Faculty of English agreed to reclassify and reshelve 8,000 books to combat 'eurocentrism'.[47]

The central Cambridge University Library has established its working group to pursue similar reclassification goals. It states that this is motivated by the 'CUL's commitments under the framework of the University's Race Equality Charter'.[48] Meanwhile, the Board of the Faculty of Classics expressed concerns that the whiteness of Plaster of Paris, used to make facsimiles of classical sculptures, may be indicative of structural racism. An open letter to the faculty called for a 'public acknowledgement of the problems of racism within Classics and the need for active anti-racist work within our discipline'.[49] In response, plaster 'casts of Roman and Greek sculptures that are on display at Cambridge University's Museum of Classical Archaeology, as well as around lecture rooms, give a "misleading impression" of the whiteness and "absence of diversity" of the ancient world'.[50] Moreover, the sculptures must now be accompanied by signs 'to turn the problem into an opportunity to draw attention to the diversity figured in the casts, to the ways in which colour has been lost and can be restored, and to the role of classical sculpture in the history of racism'.[51]

Given these widespread changes, and the public nature of the UK university system, the Higher Education Policy Institute (HEPI) found only 23% of the British public supported universities' efforts to check who is on reading lists to move away from a white, Eurocentric curriculum while centring on indigenous knowledge.[52] Jo Grady, the head of the University and College Union (UCU) argued that this was simply further evidence for the need to push on with the decolonisation agenda. 'The level of hostility towards decolonising activity in UK higher education shows just how far we have to go to tackle systemic racism.'[53] Usefully, HEPI advises that universities can simply change how they describe the push to decolonise teaching and curriculums. By nudging perceptions this way, people 'are more inclined to support changes to the curriculum when it is framed as a broadening of perspectives, rather than the removal of Western-centric viewpoints'.[54]

## Microaggressions and unconscious biases

Another key element in the drive to create a more 'inclusive and diverse' university sector has been a heightened awareness around the role that alleged covert, and often unintentional forms of racism may take and the need to identify and erase these forms of racism. The principal ways these subtle and nuanced forms of alleged racism are manifested are through 'microaggressions'. Borrowing from an influential paper on microaggressions in academia, the EHRC define these as 'brief, everyday interactions that send denigrating messages to [people of colour] because they belong to a racially minoritised group'. They continue that compared 'to more overt forms of racism, racial microaggressions are subtle and insidious, often leaving the victim confused, distressed and frustrated and the perpetrator oblivious of the offence they have caused'.[55]

Their 2019 report finds that '42% of students who experienced racial harassment during the 2018/19 academic year reported being subjected to microaggressive acts'. Importantly for universities legally, the EHRC argues that through repetition and escalation of microaggressions, those carrying out these behaviours may be breaking the 2010 Equality Act and the Public Sector Equality Duty (PSED), that imposes on public-sector bodies the legal requirement to ensure equality of opportunity between people with protected characteristics, including race.[56] Given the PSED, many universities thus carry out training courses and other forms of cultural management to root out unconscious biases and police microaggressions on campus. As such, repeated instances of microaggressions may lead to possible litigation and the reputational damage that this would likely involve for any university.

In response to the alleged widespread prevalence of racial microaggressions, many universities have outlined action plans and forms of unconscious bias training. King's College's race equality action plan has introduced 'management learning, development and support, increasing knowledge of racism, whiteness, white privilege'. It will support 'managers to make more informed, stronger decisions and combat bias'. To this end, they have developed an 'anonymous disclosure tool to cover microaggressions'.[57] Liverpool University has initiated widespread unconscious bias training, with a key milestone being all heads of department trained in unconscious bias.[58] Solent University has committed to improving 'awareness and understanding of racism, racial harassment, white privilege and microaggressions among all staff and students, including through anti-racist training'.[59]

Sheffield University has committed to addressing implicit bias through mandatory equality training programmes. Its Vice Chancellor Koen Lamberts is currently paying twenty of his students £9.34 an hour to monitor and report other staff and students for racist microaggressions to help 'change the way people think about racism'. If an alleged perpetrator suggests that the accuser is 'searching for things to be offended about' this is further evidence of racism and itself recorded as a microaggression. Lambert's microaggression monitors are there to 'help students develop skills to consider the impact of subtle but offensive comments directed at black, Asian and minority ethnic people'.[60]

Edinburgh University outlines a list of common racial microaggressions. For example, stating that your 'colour doesn't matter to me, everyone's human'. This, for example, is a form of what Edinburgh calls 'colour "blindness"' and a racist microaggression. Similarly, anybody that questions the 'lived experience' of non-white students and staff is also guilty of a racial microaggression, as well the denial of one's individual prejudice.[61] Imperial College also gives a similar example of microaggressive racism such as the Enlightenment belief that there is 'only one race, the human race'. In what they argue is indicative of the 'Myth of Meritocracy' anybody stating that they 'believe the most qualified person should get the job' is committing a racial microaggression.[62] St Andrews has introduced compulsory modules on diversity that students must pass to matriculate. Questions typically offer a choice between agree or disagree. One question asks whether acknowledging 'your personal guilt is a useful start point in overcoming unconscious bias' with those who disagree marked as incorrect. Reflecting the microaggression of 'colour blindness' another question from the course asks: 'Does equality mean treating everyone the same?' Those who respond yes are told: 'That's not right, in fact equality may mean treating people differently and in a way that is appropriate to their needs so that they have fair outcomes and equal opportunity.'[63]

## Summary

In 2019, the EHRC, the UK's preeminent body for ensuring businesses and organisations observe the 2010 Equality Act published a series of damning reports that alleged a prevalence of racism across UK campuses. These reports, coupled with the aftershocks of the killing of George Floyd in 2020 and the global rise of the Black Lives Matter (BLM) movement led to a heightened sensitivity to questions of racism on British campuses. Although originating in the United States, British universities have adopted many of the ideas and language that we see in America. The key metrics that prove this racism are a degree attainment gap between BAME and white students, the prevalence of microaggressions and an insufficient commitment on the part of academics to decolonise their teaching and curricula. Whiteness is said to be a form of malign influence on British campuses, and university leaders alongside powerful charities like Advance HE, are now seeking to lead systemic and cultural change across the UK Higher Education landscape. If politics is downstream from culture, universities remain the key tributaries of our collective ideas. As such, it is imperative that we analyse and interrogate these ideas to assess their veracity to make sure the radical changes we are seeing on British campuses and in Anglophone culture more generally are factually correct. We do so in the next chapter.

# 3

# Moral panic and illiberalism in universities

We have seen how 'woke' progressivism in the UK and the Western world argues that Western civilisation is fundamentally morally compromised and that its economic pre-eminence is based on human exploitation. The charge is that the legacy effects of this help to sustain a widespread discourse of racism that needs decolonialisation to help achieve equity. Even some of the most progressive universities are fundamentally compromised too and need wholesale structural transformation and 'decolonisation' to remove the sources of discrimination and unfairness.

This chapter challenges the view that universities are fundamentally racist and thus the empirical basis of the decolonisation agenda. Instead, I argue that the EHRC, the UUK and universities more generally have promoted a moral panic concerning racism and discrimination on UK campuses that has little bearing on reality. This moral panic has led to a profound degradation of campus life, helped to bolster the power of illiberal activists and senior university technocrats, threatened the keystone value of academic freedom, infantilised staff and students and has had broader social and political consequences for the UK.

## EHRC reports: Are universities racist?

To begin, we must conduct an analysis of the EHRC reports from 2019. These were central to the broader moral panic across UK campuses as to the prevalence of racism and discrimination. They have been cited and used by organisations like Advance HE as part of their business expansion to become the central agency responsible for university 'anti-racist' accreditation. They also underpin the UUK's decolonisation agenda. Let us unpack some of the EHRC's claims.

First, the non-white population of the UK is 18% according to the last UK census of 2021, with ethnic minority students making up 20% of the entire student population in the UK. 504,292 ethnic minority students were studying in British universities in the same academic year covered by the EHRC student surveys (2018/19).[1] Of the 1,009 students surveyed by the EHRC, 526 were ethnic minorities, 0.1% of the total UK ethnic minority student population. Beyond the one-year student survey, the broader university-wide inquiry was designed to gather evidence from a three-and-a-half-year period between the start of the 2015/16 academic year and January 2019. As we saw in the previous chapter, throughout this period, around four in ten institutions in the EHRC's university survey reported having received no complaints of racial harassment from staff; around three in ten received no reports from students. Almost one in five institutions received no complaints of racial harassment from either group.[2]

What does the above tell us? British universities employ 670,000 staff and teach 2.3 million students annually. In a three-and-a-half-year period, where 9,200,000 students passed through the UK's higher education institutions, 0.006% of students reported incidents of racial harassment to their universities. Of staff, just 0.05% made complaints. The report's authors attribute this 'under-reporting' to a lack of confidence for students and staff in their university's ability to address the problem. However, students in the EHRC's reports were asked how well they thought their university was tackling the issue of racial harassment, the results of which were overwhelmingly positive:

> One in seven (14%) students said that they felt their university was handling the issue of racial harassment very well (scores of 9–10), a further one in four (23%) felt that the university was handling the issue fairly well (scores of 7–8). Less than one in twenty (3%) students said that their university was not handling the issue well. Four in ten students (39%) felt unable to answer the question and selected 'Don't know'.[3]

Racism is a scourge and forms of racism and harassment should always be tackled robustly. However, the data above clearly indicate that the UK's universities are very far from being hotbeds of racism. Indeed, the EHRC's data corroborate universities' work to tackle racism on campus. Specifically, while 2% of ethnic minority students felt that racial harassment was a big problem and 8% somewhat of a problem, 6% did not know, 14% were neutral, and 70% ranged from a response of not particularly a problem to no problem at all.

When ethnic minority students were asked how worried they were about being personally subjected to racial harassment at their place of study, 87% responded from neutrality through to not at all worried, with the latter the largest group at 43% of the total. As such, the vast majority of ethnic minority students reported no problems and where they had reported racial harassment were happy with the outcomes. In a total of almost four years, universities across the whole of the UK had dealt with *on average one complaint of racial harassment a year*, with only 3% of those students who did report racial harassment feeling unhappy with how their universities had handled their complaints.

This is a positive story insofar as it shows that UK universities are largely free from discrimination, have robust protocols in places to deal with it and, in the thankfully tiny number of incidents where it does occur, have dealt with it in a way with which most complainants are happy. In short, it's almost exactly as one would expect from highly progressive and diverse institutions that have educated millions of young people and have a long-standing commitment to anti-discrimination.

Beyond the above, however, more fundamental problems invalidate the surveys and the methodology used. When using data based on surveys, it is common for researchers to conduct multiple samples to mitigate a range of problems, such as sensitivity analysis, regarding the questions asked. It is imperative to establish how sensitive the outputs are to input changes to be confident. In this case, how much do specific definitions, their phrasing, and the questions chosen change the overall figures? Without doing this, you don't know how sensitive your answers are to the definitions you use or the phrasing of questions. If a small difference in how you ask a question has a profound effect, or if two standard definitions produce drastically different outcomes, you have an unreliable model or an essentially contested concept.

Without this analysis, we cannot have a transparent, honest, and data-led discussion over the prevalence of racial harassment because we do not know how much of an effect various criteria or definitions have. It is hard to know what to 'do' with these data if we don't know a scientifically valid standard for attributing a racist motivation to examples used to evidence racism such as 'being ignored or excluded from conversation'. If a different criterion has a profound effect, we have a problem over concepts first and data second, which would need to be resolved. Beyond the above, there are three significant areas of the moral panic in UK universities. 'Mathiness', emotive reasoning and concept stretching.

## Mathiness

The concept of mathiness comes from the Nobel Prize-winning economist Paul Romer. It refers to emphasising statistics to push an ideological agenda by using mathematics to disguise intentions. Examples can be the redefinition of words to mean unfamiliar things, unrealistic assumptions, or the use of hypothetical conclusions to suggest they have practical significance.[4] In short, the use of mathematics/statistics to mislead, intentionally or otherwise. In the EHRC reports, there are several examples.

First, the figures for reported racial harassment are very low, so there has been an inflation of cases to generate a more prominent headline figure. For example, staff and students are divided by complaints from 2015/16 to January 2019. However, the appropriate figure would be the annual mean number quoted in tables 2.1 and 2.2 in the Racial Harassment Inquiry: A Survey of Universities. This is annual, and three times smaller than the number used in the Executive Summary. To put it another way, why divide 2019's staff and student numbers by the summation of complaints from 2015/16 to 2019?[5]

The short tract on the 'finite population correction' is more important. There is no apparent use for this section aside from an attempt to use some rather basic mathematical notation, perhaps to fool the general reader. This serves no purpose, as this report has no inferential statistical analysis. It does not present any statistical test or model that would require such a correction or make use of it. Moreover, accepting that the finite population correction makes sense if you are sampling a large proportion of the population, and offering the benefit of the doubt that some inferential statistical analysis was planned, the EHRC research is problematic as the reports take the population to equal reporting institutions.

In contrast, the actual population we care about are students and staff. Just because 89% of institutions responded doesn't mean you have data for 89% of the students and staff. Finally, throughout the report, descriptive statistics show what category of person was most likely to be the victim or the aggressor. Still, there does not appear to be an attempt to control population size. For example, if I were a policy maker, I would like to know both the general prevalence of harassment and whether the majority in a specific group is 'representative'. To say that middle-ranking staff are more at risk is likely to reflect more middle-ranking staff; a proper comparison would look at each group's 'per capita' rate.

## BAME numbers?

As we saw in the previous chapters, British universities have also been criticised for the alleged under-representation of ethnic minority staff and students. In practice, diversity tends to mean fewer white people, and more from ethnic minority backgrounds. This disparity is an important element that is being used to drive through the decolonisation agenda and a very strong push to further 'diversify' staff and students with, for example, positive racial discrimination to increase the numbers of black female senior academics.[6]

If we recall, Advance HE is the organisation responsible for the 'Race Equality Charter'. The guiding principle of the REC is that 'racial inequalities are a significant issue within higher education' and that 'UK higher education cannot reach its full potential unless it can benefit from the talents of the whole population and until individuals from all ethnic backgrounds can benefit equally from the opportunities it affords'.[7] The alleged lack of diversity among staff and students is key to sustaining these assertions. Indeed, Alison Johns, Advance HE's CEO argued that while 'not all commentators agree that there is racism in UK higher education, the evidence says otherwise – and we, as a sector, have a legal and moral duty to do something about it'. She continues that 'while black students are generally more engaged with their studies, they are consistently scored lower: 86% of white students qualify with a first or 2:1 – for black students the figure is 66.3%'. Beyond students, there is a similar disparity with staff 'where 89.1% of professors are white, and 0.7% are black; you are twice as likely to be a professor if you're a white academic than if you are black'. Dismissing critiques of her REC as part of a culture war, she insists that her organisation's is instead an evidence-based approach used to advance the equity agenda across UK campuses.[8]

However, her own organisation's data completely contradict the guiding principles used to justify its own REC, and the broader narrative that an alleged disparity therefore equals structural racism and discrimination. For example, Advance HE's own 2021 Staff Statistical Report shows a clear trend to greater diversity within the UK university sector. To quote directly: between '2003/04 and 2019/20, the proportion of all staff who were UK white steadily decreased (from 83.1% to 70.0%), while all other groups increased, most notably those from non-UK white backgrounds (from 8.3% to 14.6%)'. They go on to show that during 'this same period, the proportion of all staff who were UK black, Asian and minority ethnic increased from 4.8% to 8.5%, and the proportion of non-UK black, Asian and minority ethnic staff increased from 3.8% to 7.0%'.[9]

The non-white UK population is 18%. The figures thus show a disproportionate *over-representation* of BAME staff across the UK sector, and a very clear trend of ever-greater BAME staff numbers year on year. These numbers are very stark in certain subject areas. For example, 'areas with the highest proportions of UK black, Asian and minority ethnic staff were clinical dentistry (25.1%), chemical engineering (21.7%) and electrical, electronic and computer engineering (21.7%)', while BAME non-UK 'academics working in electrical, electronic and computer engineering' comprise 57% of staff and almost 47% in business studies. Even among the most senior of staff at professorial level, 'there was a small difference between the proportions of white and black, Asian and minority ethnic staff who were professors (11.6% and 9.5% respectively)'. When we disaggregate the BAME category, however, there are notable differences. Specifically, '17.0% of UK Chinese academics were professors compared with just 4.0% of UK black academics'.[10]

Regarding senior managers and administrators, the data again show a diversity that is commensurate with population demographics. Senior managers from the UK academic population make up 1.3% of all UK academics. Of this 1.3%, senior managers from the UK white population were 0.9% with UK black, Asian and minority ethnic academics 0.4%. Moreover, the median pay gap between UK white and UK black, Asian and minority ethnic staff is zero.[11]

How about the student population? In 2021, 25.3% of students at UK universities identified as black, Asian and minority ethnic.[12] This represents an astonishing rise in diversity among students, with the 2021 477,355 UK domiciled students identified as black, Asian and minority ethnic representing an 82.3% increase from 2003/04 numbers.[13] In 2021, 24.6% of Oxford's intake were black or minority ethnic students. In 2019, data show that the proportion of 19 to 25-year-olds across the UK was 80.6% white and 19.4% BME. However, BME students made up almost 29% of the total intake at British universities in the same year, including over 25% at the elite Russell Group.[14]

Advance HE is an organisation at the forefront of leading cultural change of 'diversity and inclusion' by selling its REC as the answer to alleged widespread racial discrimination across the university sector. However, their data analysis shows the opposite of what they claim: a rich diversity of BAME staff and students that on a demographic basis is mostly over-represented, and at staff levels across the seniority ranges. The narrative underpinning the 'Race Equality Charter' is totally at odds with the reality and a reality that Advance HE's own data show.

## Conceptual apartheid

Aside from these data, the decolonisation agenda to diversify staff rests on an odd assumption but one common in the social-justice movement. In what we might call a correspondence theory of knowledge, primacy is placed on the correspondence between the immutable identity characteristics of a teacher and student. As such, diversity is seen as a panacea to a problem that rests on an assumption that the optimal way to learn is to be taught by somebody of your own racial identity.

First, this implies an assumed affinity between teacher and student based on race or another form of identity. As such, social justice is achieved through diversifying teachers based on immutable identity characteristics. However, surely what is important in the relationship is the veracity of the information and knowledge being imparted and the quality of the teaching? Why and in what ways is the ethnicity or background of those taking part in knowledge exchange relevant? Do the laws of physics somehow change depending on the ethnicity of the professor and her students? Of course not.

Second, racialising knowledge in this way is a form of identity imposition that underplays diversity. For example, by coding staff and students as black, people from a range of diverse backgrounds, from the Caribbean to Nigeria, are all lumped into one generic 'black' category. The same could be said for white staff and students, with those from the UK coded the same as those from, for example, Russia; i.e. from very different cultures and historical traditions. Why would a white professor born and educated in the former Soviet Union have more cultural affinity with a white British student than a black British professor teaching white undergraduates, born in the UK? This correspondence theory of knowledge racialises knowledge exchange and creates a form of intellectual apartheid where the colour of one's skin take precedence over one's own individuality, cultural identification and lived experience.

Third, and as a result of the above, the correspondence theory of knowledge is explicitly ideological. Drawing from intersectional theories of identity, it imposes this schema on the world and thus privileges its own priorities (identity) over other values such as excellence, hard work or merit. Indeed, these values have come under explicit attack by ideologues as evidence of white supremacy.[15] There are several key dangers with this approach. Not only does this patronise BAME students, but it also runs the risk of undermining achievement by attributing certain values along racial lines. All of humanity's advances are based on the application of intelligence, hard work, making the right choices and so on. Moreover, an optimal and functional society is one where those most qualified for a job get to do that job, be it road sweeper or brain surgeon. It is both patronising and dangerous to the advancement of minority groups to peddle the fantasy that a personal ethos of victimhood, self-pity and grievance (absent genuine injustice) is a better accelerant of personal advancement than application, self-discipline and hard work.

Fourth, it is consistently shown that the lowest participation rates at universities are young men from white working-class backgrounds. If we accept the arguments of the decolonial movement, and if we value consistency, presumably this means that to encourage more equal outcomes for this historically disadvantaged group, we should insist that only white working-class male professors should teach white boys from working-class backgrounds? This is the malign and illiberal logical conclusion of the correspondence theory of knowledge.

## Attainment gap?

How about the alleged degree attainment gap that is a key element also driving the decolonisation agenda in UK universities?

According to the Higher Education Statistics Agency (HESA) 29% of white students attained first-class degrees in 2017/18, while 13.5% of black students did. As we saw in the previous chapter, this disparity has led to accusations of racism and racial inequality. The claim is that by decolonising the curriculum, you make it somehow more in tune with BAME students' needs, which allegedly consistently underperform in their degree results because of an overly Eurocentric white curriculum.

However, the data show that 21% of Asians and 25% of mixed-race students got firsts. When we move down the scale to a 2:1 UK degree classification, 47% of whites, 42% of blacks and 44% of Asian and 49% of mixed-race students got 2:1s.[16] If, as has been asserted, differential attainment indicates racism, why do mixed-race and Asian students get the same number of firsts as white students? Similarly, how do we explain that when it comes to 2:1s, the pass rates for all students are comparable?

Similarly, the available data on student degree attainment show a very close correlation between A-level results and degree outcome.[17] For example, of the students entering university with the highest grades of three A*, 52% of Asians, 58% of black and 59% of white students left with a first-class degree. Of those with the lowest A-level grades below CCD, the numbers are comparable: 17% of Asians, 10% of black and 17% of white students with the lowest grades achieved a first-class degree.[18] The data also show that the proportion of students with first and upper second-class degrees is largely comparable across all ethnicities. Of those with the highest A-level results, 92% of Asian, 96% black and white students left with firsts or upper second-class degrees.

To believe that racial discrimination accounts for what are in many cases statistically insignificant differences between students of different ethnicities, we would have to believe several things at once. First, the racism at universities is so insidious that it differentiates between races to the extent that it does not discriminate against mixed-race or Asian students whose results are comparable with white students. Second, this specifically anti-black racism somehow does not carry over even against black students when we control for qualifications on entry to universities, with all students with the highest grades and lowest grades having broadly comparable outcomes in their respective degree results, irrespective of ethnicity.

Third, even among the 'black' group, this term does not control for very important differences between Afro-Caribbean and African heritage students. The data clearly show that across a range of metrics, what is treated as a largely undifferentiated 'black' group by Advance HE, UUK and so on disguises important educational data. In pre-tertiary education for example (and when the latest data are available) over 10% of black Caribbean pupils were temporarily excluded in 2019, white British at 6%, while black African at 4%.[19] That is, within the 'black' category, Afro-Caribbean black kids were excluded at more than double the rate of African black kids from British schools. This interesting difference carries over into tertiary education. In terms of progression to university by Free School Meal (FSM) status (a lead measure of relative poverty), 66% of black African females and 51% of black African males progressed to university while only 44% of black female Caribbean and 24% of black Caribbean males progressed.[20] In short, within the 'black' category are very clear differences.

This inference is supported by the fact that while 10.7% of black children now go to the top universities, only 5.4% of black Caribbean pupils do, compared with 13.2% of black African pupils. If we disaggregate on sex, 3.5% of black Caribbean boys go to top universities compared with 10.2% of black African boys.[21] These are very wide differences among a group that is often treated as a largely undifferentiated mass within a specific 'black' category.

Fourth, this racism seemingly entirely disappears when it applies to students who achieve an upper-second degree and below (i.e. the vast majority) with little to no statistical difference between students from different ethnicities across the range of those not qualifying with the highest award of a first-class degree. Fifth, this racism somehow discriminates, even though exams and essays are marked anonymously by examiners, with the marker having no idea of the identity or race of those they're marking.

Sixth, despite the claim that the history of colonialism and 'colonial epistemologies' help to explain seemingly differential educational outcomes between white and BAME students, many BAME students from former British colonies such as India and Hong Kong have some of the highest educational outcomes of all. These educational outcomes then translate into earnings (which we will examine in more detail below). If colonialism and the British Empire are responsible for structural racism measured by alleged disparities, how is it that students from these countries have some of the highest educational outcomes in UK higher education and are demographically over-represented among the academic population? Indeed, given the logic of the decolonial critique, shouldn't students from Hong Kong have the worst outcomes (as opposed to some of the best), given the fact that the territory only formally passed from British 'subjugation' in 1997?

Lastly, one of the most persecuted groups in human history are Jews. From imposed exile in ancient history to the enormity of the Holocaust, anti-semitism has been all too tragically common throughout history. Indeed, it is still all too common across the British university system: for example, the 2022 dismissal of the National Union of Student's President Shaima Dallali over anti-semitism.[22] Despite this millennia-long

history of persecution, Jews are the highest educated of all
of the world's religious groups, and are often leaders in their
respective academic fields.[23] For example, despite compromis-
ing a mere 0.2% of the world's population, they account for
24% of all Nobel Prizes since the year 2000.[24] If the equation
was as simple as that the legacy of racism leads to sub-optimal
educational outcomes, how on earth can we explain the academic success of one of history's most persecuted minorities?

What is a more plausible explanation between the obvious
disconnect between the data and the dominant narrative that
universities are hotbeds of racial discrimination that need now
to be decolonised?

What has happened is a form of very poor 'univariate'
social-science analysis. What does this mean? When trying
to explain something, in this case a degree attainment gap,
we need to understand the range of variables that may affect
the thing we wish to learn more about in order to understand
which variables have the most salience. In social science, this
is called a multivariate analysis, i.e. controlling for multiple
variables. Thus, even if we accept the argument of degree disparity between different ethnic groups, without controlling for
a range of other salient factors that may influence outcomes
we cannot simply state that one variable (racism) explains this
outcome or conduct what is little more than a simplistic univariate analysis.

We would not even do this on something as simple as the
failure of a cake recipe, whereby, for example, it failed to rise
once cooked. We would naturally examine what measures we
used, the amounts of flour we put in, the temperature of the
oven, the quality of our ingredients and so on. A bad cook
would simply blame one of what are in fact multiple elements
that go into making a good cake. Now imagine we extrapo
late from this admittedly frivolous example to examine the
complexity of the British Higher Education system, which has
taught a diverse range of millions of students and is composed

of thousands of staff across the entire country and drawn from across the globe. These students all have different life stories, educational backgrounds, familial structures, socio-economic positions, and their own agency. How odd that these things are all discounted to alight upon one explanation of many that fits the activist's political agenda: racism.

## Identifying the variables

What are some obvious variables that may explain differential attainment between students?

First, most black students come from state schools and state-school students overall, black, and white, tend to do less well at university than their private-school counterparts. School experience and prior attainment play a crucial role in determining degree outcomes. As schools have undergone changes in institutional and curricular arrangements over the years, students may have similar or identical qualifications but vastly different educational experiences. Depending on the chosen degree subject, prior school experience (separate from qualifications) can have a significant impact on outcomes and retention rates. To fully understand disparities and make informed decisions in education policy, it is important to take these broader context factors into account.

In 2020, for example, the proportion of A-level students given top grades reached a record high. Data from regulator Ofqual showed the increase in A grades was 50% higher in independent schools than in secondary comprehensives.[25] This is especially pertinent given the above data on the correlation between entry grades and exit degree attainment. It is likely that black and white kids who go to the same kinds of schools (often inner-city state schools) and then the same universities will leave with the same degree results, i.e. this is about socio-economic class rather than race.

Second, degree choice has a significant bearing on degree results, with attainment gaps wider in non-science and science subjects. The difference between BAME and white degree outcomes in the subject of education and teaching was 15.9%, whereas in general and other sciences it was 0.6% and in medicine and dentistry 0.8%, i.e. statistically insignificant.[26] Moreover, the trend line between the alleged degree-awarding gap is closing, even among white and black students (those with the largest disparity). If degree attainment is indicative of some form of racial discrimination, then we must also accept that academics in education and teaching are inherently more racist than their science colleagues, given very significant awarding gaps between those from different ethnicities. Perhaps we should decolonise education, but leave medicine and dentistry alone?

Third, the Office for National Statistics (ONS) shows that in the six years to 2020, the percentage of graduates who got a first-class or 2:1 degree went up in every ethnic group, with the biggest increases in the black ethnic group (from 50.8% to 65.8%) and other ethnic groups (from 62.4% to 75.1%). On the other hand, the smallest increase was in the white ethnic group (from 77.1% to 85.9%), with the percentage gap between white and black graduates getting a first-class or 2:1 degree going down from 26.3% to 20.0% between 2014 to 2020.[27]

Fourth, black students make up more than a third of all first-year undergraduates. Moreover, given the concentration of ethnic minorities within major urban conurbations such as London, there is a disproportionate representation of BAME students at a small number of institutions. For example, London Metropolitan, the University of East London and the University of West London all have the largest black-student populations. For all BAME students (including mixed and Asian) the top universities are City University, Bradford and the London Metropolitan University.[28] The majority of these are former polytechnics of the 'post-92' group of universities, which historically award fewer firsts than the more 'prestigious' Russell Group universities. Again, any basic multivariate analysis would have picked up these variables and controlled them, in order to ascertain the veracity of the charge of anti-black racism and structural discrimination. It is also worth asking: how can British universities institute such radical changes within their teaching and research when they are supposed to be evidence-led centres of excellence and in receipt of billions of pounds of taxpayers' money?

## Microaggressions and emotive reasoning

Arguably more important than the mechanics of the data analysis are the qualitative issues involved in sustaining the narrative of racism and moral panic in UK universities.

First, in the EHRC reports, no disaggregation was undertaken between ethnic groups regarding the 'perpetrator' of the alleged racist incidents. This is especially troubling when the UK has very high international staff and students, who inevitably come from cultures with different traditions around race relations. As such, and even though the reports noted white students as victims of racism, universities have responded to the EHRC reports with training programmes aimed at 'fixing' the 'problem' in the white–ethnic majority (where racism is defined as white privilege, whiteness as structural racism, white fragility, etc.) but have not controlled for which populations are carrying out harassment or microaggressions. The data as presented allow for this inherent majority/minority narrative, with no disaggregation or nuance.

Second, there is considerable conceptual stretching involved in grouping overt racial harassment with microaggressions. These microaggressions form most of the evidence base for the allegations of widespread racism on UK campuses.

The theory of microaggressions originally comes from an influential paper 2007 by Derald Wing Sue, but it is notoriously elastic and unscientific.[29] For example, in one instance researchers solicited reports of academic microaggressions from African American graduate students. The authors identified both as withholding criticism from supervisees and providing them with tough criticism as evidence of microaggressions.[30] Microaggressions are a classic case of emotive reasoning: 'I feel that something was racist, and my feelings are evidence of that racism. Therefore, the act was racist.'

This highly subjective 'eye of the beholder' theory of racism is deeply problematic, since it disregards the essential question of intent of an alleged perpetrator and the perception bias of the alleged 'victim', whose offence is based on a form of what cognitive-behavioural therapists call mind-reading. For example, Sue argued that the question 'Where were you born?' directed at Asian Americans was a microaggression. It reflects the assumption that recipients are 'different from, less than, and could not possibly be, "real" Americans'. However, leaping to this inference without attempting to check one's perceptions constitutes a form of mind-reading. In a very real sense, microaggression theory is an unscientific and uncharitable form of clairvoyance that codes everyday interactions in a paranoid and ideologically loaded way that is self-confirmative. Moreover, these theories have degraded campus cultures through illiberal forms of psychological policing such as unconscious bias to root out alleged 'microaggressions' in the minds of staff and students.

Another obvious problem is the clear capacity for activist staff and students to weaponise these amorphous forms of mind-reading either to gain individual career acceleration or to generate wider forms of socio-political change. In the latter case, Equality, Diversity, and Inclusion (EDI) bureaucracies have grown in power and size across the university sector, especially since the rise of the BLM movement following the killing of George Floyd in America. These bureaucracies exist to police the implementation of the UK's 2010 Equality Act, and the broader Public Sector equality duty (PSED). This law mandates public-sector bodies to have due regard to promoting equality of opportunity between people with protected characteristics, including race. As these EDI bureaucracies have grown in scale and size, so have their power within universities. Data show that the UK has seen a 58% increase in diversity and inclusion roles since 2015, most of which are at the most senior level. Today, 'UK organisations employ twice as many D&I professionals per 10,000 employees than any country in the world and have the second largest number of D&I professionals globally, behind the US.'[31]

In the case of weaponisation of this moral panic by activists, as we saw in previous chapters, post-colonial and decolonial theories are explicitly committed to deep-rooted political change and 'social justice'. It is thus unsurprising that these movements use these theories, nascent EDI bureaucracies and appeals to authority to impose the kinds of changes we saw in the last chapter. This is what Campbell and Manning call a 'victimhood culture' that is now increasingly prevalent on campuses. They argue that this victimhood culture is a 'form of social control in which the aggrieved collect and publicise accounts of intercollective offences, making the case that relatively minor slights are part of a larger pattern of injustice and that those who suffer them are socially marginalised and deserving of sympathy'.[32]

We thus end up in a place where even basic human interactions are now being policed and coded in highly authoritarian and illiberal ways. This alliance between activism and top-down policing is clear. For example, the UUK's guidance states that universities need to increase 'staff and students' understanding of racism, racial harassment and microaggressions and white privilege, through training developed from an anti-racist perspective'. This needs to be moved beyond psychological audits such as 'unconscious bias training' to setting 'targets for completion and carefully evaluating all training activities to ensure they have the desired effect'.[33]

To give a sense of how all-encompassing the definitions of microaggressions are, the EHRC give several examples of interactions between white and BAME staff and students. Remember, these form the key empirical basis for the charge of ubiquitous racism in UK universities and thus the drive for greater EDI bureaucracies and micro-management of campus cultures.

Some of the examples given include the apparent reluctance to share a lift with somebody, not getting an important email, the fact that the UK voted to leave the European Union, which has allegedly 'introduced a cold wind into universities that has reduced civility and increased harassment' or not being invited to lunch or a coffee break. Indeed, the concept is so wide that the EHRC argued that an academic's body language and demeanour can be taken as evidence of a racial microaggression. When talking to non-white students, academics will allegedly 'use certain phrases that they wouldn't use with your other Caucasian peers. There is a change in the attitude when they address you. And you can feel it.'[34] This bizarre form of policing has very real consequences and sits at the heart of even the UK's leading universities. For example, former Vice-Chancellor of Cambridge, Stephen Toope committed his institution to creating a 'safe, welcoming and inclusive community'. To that end, an anonymous online reporting system was set up to report staff for microaggressions, one of which included raising 'an eyebrow when black students or staff speak' and was only amended when Toope's decision faced public scrutiny.[35] It is unclear how an anonymous portal for reporting fellow students' raised eyebrows helped inculcate a welcoming and inclusive community.

Similarly, an Advance HE training package on microaggressions lists a series of bizarre examples. For example, if a white academic dares to question the integrity or 'impact of institutional racism' on UK campuses it is because of their white guilt and 'fear of a new order (black planet)'. Similarly, allegedly not being served at a 'bar/restaurant while others were served all around me' is another example of a microaggression.[36]

Importantly, these forms of emotive microaggressions are said to be possibly more damaging than the more widespread and overt racism we may have found in the UK decades ago. Professor Binna Kandola OBE is one of the UK's key specialists on microaggressions and what he calls 'micro-incivilities'. His book, *Racism at Work: The Danger of Indifference* has been endorsed by such leading UK politicians as former Conservative Health Secretary, Matt Hancock.[37] In his 2019 keynote address at Advance HE's annual BME Leadership in Higher Education Summit, Kandola outlined the logic. Modern racism is very different from the older and more overt forms of racism. 'It is subtle, oblique and indirect in its manifestation, yet its impact on the people on the receiving end can be just as devastating, and sometimes more so.' More insidiously hardly a week goes by 'without another story about racism on university campuses'. He asks, 'what if the people joining in the chorus of outrage were racist themselves, but in more difficult to detect ways?' He then goes on to list indicative examples of racial microaggressions and closet white supremacy. These include not praising somebody, giving feedback to somebody late, criticising somebody or not 'giving someone eye contact' when talking to them.[38] One dreads to think what may happen should somebody not only fail to maintain eye contact but simultaneously raise their eyebrows!

As such, in the modern university sector, we have seen both a seemingly manufactured moral panic and the growth of EDI bureaucracies to deal with what are often phantom issues of racism on UK campuses. This is not to deny that racism exists. Universities should be places of equal opportunity and totally free from discrimination. Where these things are found to exist overtly, they should be robustly combatted. However, the data clearly show that UK universities are diverse, inclusive, and welcoming institutions from people all over the world. Moreover, in the thankfully tiny number of racist incidents reported, the overwhelming majority of staff and students who reported these incidents felt they had been treated fairly. The data clearly show an incredibly diverse campus culture, with BAME staff and students over-represented on a per capita basis. I have shown that the primary evidential basis for the charges of widespread racism cannot be sustained when we look at the data, control for multiple variables or reject an unscientific theory of micro-aggressive clairvoyance that struggles so hard to find discrimination that it sees it in everyday and entirely innocent human interactions and behaviours such as raising an eyebrow or taking the stairs.

Universities, like many other Western institutions, have adopted what has become a common trope of progressivism that conflates equal outcomes with equal opportunities, whereby unequal outcomes are said to be indicative of an underlying system of discrimination. Like the USSR, social 'justice' is thus achieved by a redistributive agent (the state, university administrators, etc.) needing to intervene to impose equal outcomes. This conception shifts debates from an examination of underlying processes, which allow humans to participate equally (equal opportunity) to one of top-down imposition to achieve outcome parity, usually by a technocratic elite. In later chapters we will examine what motivates these technocrats. I have shown clearly that British universities, at least in relation to the participation of all ethnic groups, remain commendably diverse. However, for now, let us assume that disparity does in fact equal discrimination. What do the data show?

## Universities: The white working class

When we examine the data in relation to equality, stark disadvantages are exposed, most notably by young adults from the white working class, and in particular young men. Given the toxic ideology now inherent within universities, that castigates the white majority and pushes a factually inaccurate moral panic that further castigates 'whiteness' and alleged white privilege, the prognosis does not look good for promoting equality and inclusion and this is a moral and leadership failure on the part of universities.

For example, at our most selective universities, only 5% of disadvantaged young people enrol, compared with the national average of 12%. Even if they do get in, young working-class people struggle to stay, with an 8.8% dropout rate, compared with 6.3% of their peers from better-off families.

Part-time students from lower-income backgrounds have dropped by a massive 42% over the past six years. ONS figures show that the historically low entry rate into higher education of white pupils from state schools has been this way every single year since 2006, while the biggest increase in entry rates between 2006 and 2018 was among black pupils, at 19.6 percentage points (from 21.6% to 41.2%); the smallest increase was among white pupils, at 7.7 percentage points (from 21.8% to 29.5%).

The latest data on widening participation reinforce this depressing picture. A child on free school meals (FSM) is the leading indicator of deprivation but this does not equally impact all ethnic groups. In its 2021 report, the UK Education Select Committee concluded that the:

> proportion of white British pupils who were FSM-eligible starting higher education by the age of 19 in 2018/19 was 16.0%, the lowest of any ethnic group other than traveller of Irish heritage and Gypsy/Roma. FSM-eligible white other pupils had

a participation rate of 37.2%, FSM-eligible Chinese pupils had a participation rate of 72.8%, and FSM-eligible pupils from a black African background had a participation rate of 59.0%. FSM-eligible pupils from a black Caribbean background had a participation rate of 31.8%.[39]

There are multiple reasons why this is the case. The Committee argued that '"aspirations" and "culture" are recurring themes in the debate about how to help the white working class'. The committee also identified 'an "immigrant paradigm" that leads some families to place greater value on education, while multi-generational disadvantage, particularly among white (and black Caribbean) families, has inculcated feelings of hopelessness and powerlessness to break the cycle of poverty'. The ONS concludes that 'pupils from the Chinese ethnic group had the highest entry rate into higher education from 2006 to 2020', while 'in every year from 2007 to 2020, white pupils had the lowest entry rate into higher education – the percentage of state-school pupils aged 18 accepted into college or university'.[40]

A report by NEON, an organisation trying to address these issues, concluded that less than 20% of UK universities have set targets in their Access and Participation Plans for white students from low-income neighbourhoods. This is despite often being situated in areas of significant deprivation. Recognising the dysfunctional nature of incentives and governance of our Higher Education system, NEON state that in 'the context of the outcome driven approach to access and participation being promoted by the regulator for HE, the Office for Students, if something is not seen as an outcome or target then it will not be prioritised'.[41]

Tellingly, these educational disadvantages have significant real-world effects. ONS data show Chinese, Indian, and mixed or multiple ethnicity employees all have higher median hourly pay than white British employees, with

Chinese employees earning 30.9% more than white British employees.[42]

There is also a gender dimension. The Higher Education Policy Institute's latest survey of gender participation rates across degrees of all ranges and shows a long-term trend of declining male participation. Mary Curnock Cook, Chief Executive of UCAS, states that 'young women are now 35% more likely to go to university than men. If this differential growth carries on unchecked, then girls born this year will be 75% more likely to go to university than their male peers'.[43] HESA data show that in 2021, 214,415 women and 152,602 men gained degrees in UK universities, a sex ratio of over 58% in favour of women. In every single subject except for engineering, computing, architecture, physical sciences and mathematics women dominate, some incredibly disproportionately such as education at 77%, psychology at 82%, subjects allied to medicine at 79% and law at 64%.[44]

## Universities as racist elite institutions

What can we conclude from the above? University leaders and self-interested businesses like Advance HE, which sell 'equality' audits to university leaders, have argued that disparities between ethnic groups and lack of diversity of campuses are indicative of underlying forms of racism and discrimination. I have examined the data in detail in this chapter. Most ethnic minorities in the UK are represented well and above their respective demographic population across the university sector; there is thankfully very little racism on UK campuses and, where it does raise its head, is dealt with robustly. Instead, activists, backed up by self-interested business charities like Advance HE, which sells its auditing to universities, and compliant and often fearful university leaders, have endorsed a racial moral panic that is leading to the radical transformation of the UK higher education sector.

This has been done on the basis of dodgy statistics, absurd theories that amount to little more than a form of clairvoyance and racial conspiracies of an all-pervasive ideology of 'whiteness' and the collective racial guilt of white people.

This is especially troubling, as the one group that has consistently been under-represented across the UK university sector is that of white working-class young adults. Not only is this under-representation consistent over many years, but most universities have also not even bothered to draw up inclusion plans to address these forms of systemic discrimination. Moreover, where equality bureaucracies exist in universities, they are driven by an ideology focused almost exclusively on race, sexuality and gender (invariably focused on women), but not on class – the lead indicator of one's life chances and predictor of success. In short, universities have knowingly endorsed racist ideas of collective guilt, which further stigmatise the one group that is consistently under-represented across the entire sector, all based on a view of history that paints the UK as irredeemably racist and that now needs to recompense ethnic minorities. We examine this history in the next chapter.

# 4

# History reclaimed

Having examined the arguments used to sustain the moral panic of racism on UK campuses, this chapter considers the theoretical and historical arguments deployed by decolonial and identity politics theorists. These arguments posit the malign nature of the Enlightenment and reject any notion of truth, objectivity, or the utility of rational adjudication between competing truth claims. By extension, Western civilisation itself is cast as beyond the pale. As Delgado and Stefancic argue, decolonial theorists inspired by CRT seek to deconstruct Western society, including 'the very foundations of the liberal order, including equality theory, legal reasoning, Enlightenment rationalism, and neutral principles of constitutional law'.[1]

In the first part of this chapter, I will argue for the value of science and truth. I do this by contrasting the postmodern emphasis on social construction with scientific realism, which offers us a valuable way to think about these deeper philosophical issues. Having established the value of scientific realism, I examine some 'counter-histories' of the West, including slavery, colonialism and the West's role in these global processes. These counter-histories are essential, as the moral power of the decolonial arguments is based on a one-sided view of British history. This view casts the UK as deeply compromised, given its role in colonialism and slavery, and provides the moral impetus for the decolonial deconstruction of British institutions. However, as Black has argued, this is a 'highly critical and somewhat ahistorical account of empire and, more particularly, the British Empire, prevails in political discussion; education, higher education in particular; colonial and post-colonial literature; and the media'.[2] I think this one-sided view replicates many of the faults that the decolonial theorists argue lie with the UK, namely an overly Eurocentric view of history that does not pay sufficient attention to the agency of the non-European world and its role in world history.

## Defending science and reason

As we saw in previous chapters, postmodernists and, by extension, most identity politics theorists draw on social constructivist epistemology. Social constructivists argue that all human knowledge is 'socially constructed' from extant cultural raw materials, and we cannot know anything outside our shared cultural frames of reference. This means that they reject any notion of truth or objectivity that exists 'out there', as all meaning is 'internal' to human perception.

Foucault and Derrida extended this insight to examine what they argued were the dominant discourses that framed our understanding of things, often negatively. Foucault argued that all knowledge has implicit power relationships imbued within it. Knowledge is not 'innocent'. Instead, it frames understandings in ways that have immense implications that are independent of what these understandings attempt to describe. For example, as a gay man, Foucault was acutely aware of how the discourse on homosexuality had changed historically, and he traced this through the ancient history of Greece to the present day; from its celebration to its medicalisation into what is today a far more liberal perspective on homosexuality – to the extent that it is celebrated within the UK as 'Pride' month every year. The critical insight is that though homosexual love has remained a constant across different historical cultures, how it has been understood (socially constructed) has changed.

Similarly, Derrida argued that Western philosophy, and by extension Western culture, is composed of hierarchically organised binaries such as man/woman, civilised/primitive, Western/non-Western and so on. One part of the dyad was seen as better and superior. Decolonial and post-colonial theorists took these ideas and argued that these discourses permeate Western civilisation and have huge legacy effects in the present day. These theorists' political goal is to establish the radical contingency of knowledge and deconstruct dominant or 'hegemonic' ways of constructing knowledge. By doing this, Western civilisation's 'Eurocentric' self-belief and confidence would be undermined and, by extension, Western political hegemony.[3] It is precisely these kinds of theoretical ideas that decolonial activists are deploying on UK campuses and university bureaucrats endorsing when expounding the need to decolonise their institutions.

As such, the historical telos of universities as depositories of our collective cultural wisdom and knowledge is thus changed from forms of debate and free speech to those of multiple truths and power plays to impose dominance. In this way, the universities and those academics within them are transformed from fallible but authoritative judges and teachers of the sum of human knowledge to being part of a broader political struggle between a binary of oppressed versus the oppressors.

In the next section of this chapter, I argue against this dominant social constructivism. Instead, I outline scientific realism and the importance of ontology (the study of being) over epistemology (what we know or feel).

## The importance of science and ontology

As outlined, social constructivism is primarily concerned with questions of knowledge, how humans come to understand the world and the forms of power involved in those processes. In short, it emphasises epistemology or how we know what we know. In contrast to this approach, scientific realism argues for the importance of ontology. This is the notion that being or reality is 'ontologically before knowing and, therefore, understanding the nature of an object of research – ontology precedes a consideration of how the researcher will get to know it (more deeply) – epistemology'.[4] This emphasis on ontology is important.

First, as Sayer has argued, the postmodernist form of judgemental relativism 'appears to have the virtue of being egalitarian and open-minded', but this elides the normative belief that 'because everyone is or should be regarded as equal, the epistemological status of their beliefs must also be equal'.[5] In short, it takes the laudable moral goal of human equality and applies it to the status of different beliefs where all exist in the form of judgement-free horizontalism.

This form of extreme relativism means we can never judge the veracity of beliefs, and the quest for knowledge and truth merely becomes a smokescreen for the imposition of power. We can see this judgemental relativism very clearly in the theories covered in previous chapters. The movement to decolonise 'white, Eurocentric' worldviews and institutions is not done based on these theories or worldviews being empirically or factually wrong. Instead, activists impose decolonisation as part of a counter-power move to push back against what they claim is knowledge power plays of historically tainted thinkers and institutions. In short, if all knowledge is relative, it becomes politically acceptable to impose your agenda in the name of social justice and a form of restorative activism. Decolonisation is thus an explicitly political power play.

This, in turn, transforms the academic social contract. It moves from a process whereby the sum of human knowledge improves in terms of its capacity to explain the world to a form of radical political deconstruction underpinned by an ethical claim that this is justified to compensate for the legacy effects of the alleged perfidiousness of Western civilisation. The assertion that all human knowledge is equally valid and the university is a site of power contestation makes it easier to understand the abandonment of fundamental academic principles, not least that of academic freedom; itself often portrayed as a conspiracy on the part of bigots to justify discrimination and ideas that may run contrary to those of the progressive 'woke' Left.[6] Aside from the obvious fact that if all knowledge is relative, why should we subscribe to the assertions of the decolonisation critique itself, this form of unbounded judgemental relativism abandons any notion of reality or truth for a seeming endless play on meaning, identity and power that is transforming the university system. The fact that the custodians of our precious universities would allow this to happen speaks to a larger collapse of authority and confidence across the Western world.

More broadly, to the extent that humanity advances based on a process of optimising what works as opposed to what makes us feel good, this deepening social constructivist worldview poses an existential threat to the very foundations of Western civilisation. It increasingly dominates our cultural meta-narratives. For example, debates on gender self-identification explicitly call upon this social constructivism whereby gender as a social construct takes precedence over the biological reality of sex differences.[7] This is similar in the 'fat acceptance movement' that seeks to normalise obesity, and that enjoys growing academic support.[8] Similarly, the advocacy for 'indigenous' knowledge or the castigation of white, Eurocentric curricula explicitly invokes judgemental relativism where all ideas are said to exist on an equal plane, regardless of their integrity.

This elevation of perceptions and emotions also undergirds the emphasis on microaggressions, where one's feelings take priority over facts. These ideas have profound implications for human wellbeing and social cohesion. From the normalisation of autogynephilia and its implications for women's safety, the growing prevalence of cancers and diabetes or the increasing illiberal policing of basic human interactions, the deleterious social outcomes of judgemental relativism are clearer day by day.

In contrast, scientific realism posits the mind's independence from the world. Scientific realism is the view that the scientific theories we have are approximately true, or at least aim to be true, and that the unobservable entities and structures postulated by these theories exist in some form. Scientific realism is based on the idea that the world is an objective and independent reality, and that our scientific theories are our best means of understanding and describing this reality. According to scientific realism, scientific theories do not simply describe our current observations and measurements, but rather they describe the underlying structure and patterns of the world that give rise to these observations and measurements.

Scientific realism holds that our scientific theories are not merely convenient instruments for predicting and controlling the world, but rather they are our best attempt at understanding the world as it really is. Indeed, this makes it a realist theory: it posits the existence of a reality that is 'out there'. Given that the world has properties that exist independently of human knowledge and remain 'true' independently of what we may believe about these things, the models we adopt to explain reality are also bounded. For example, we can believe in the capacity of human beings to fly by flapping their arms. Still, the mind-independent existence of gravity means that no matter how hard we may flap or believe in human flight, those beliefs can never be true. Similarly, we may assume that a biological man can proclaim himself a woman (and genuinely think he is a woman). Still, that belief does not change the reality and scientific truth of biological sex differences.

Importantly, this claim for the mind independence of the world, or ontological realism, is not an assertion that the objective world presents itself to us in an unmediated form. This is a form of naive realism or common-sense realism that argues that our perceptions give us direct and accurate knowledge of the external world. According to naive realism, the world is exactly as it appears to us, and our senses provide us with a direct and unmediated connection to the world.

Instead, all human knowledge is relative but, given the mind's independence of the world, it is possible to build conceptual models and make reasonable judgements about their truth insofar as those models approximate to that reality. 'Ontological realism and epistemological relativism are conditions for rational truth-judgements. On the one hand, without independent reality, truth claims would be meaningless. Truth claims have to be about something.'[9]

This realist mind independence of the world sets boundaries on our contingent theories of it (or why humans cannot fly or change biological sex through self-declaration). It also operationalises a form of 'bridging' judgemental rationalism that allows the adjudication of different truth claims. Because of the mind-independent properties of the world 'out there', some truth claims (that remain relative) about that world are 'truer' than others. As such, the worth and value of a specific understanding of the world are not decided by the identity of the progenitor of those ideas but by their rational integrity in describing the phenomenon to which they are directed. Epistemological relativism (distinct from postmodernist judgemental relativism) claims that all human knowledge is relative, fallible, context-dependent, and bounded by reality. It is never set in stone, but advances as our understandings of the world improve.[10] More broadly, this is why academic freedom and open enquiry are central to the advance of human civilisation:

they are the foundational values that allow contestation of the always contingent and fallible sum of human knowledge that is itself an iterative process of unfolding understanding. As such, the loss of these precious values is an existential threat to Western civilisation.

## The Eurocentric nature of decolonial history

This turns the decolonisation critique on its head. For example, a leading South African decolonisation advocate, Siyanda Makaula, argues that scientists' appeal to universal applicability is problematic. Scientists 'often hide behind their disciplines' putative universality – that a cell is a cell, whether it belongs to an African or a European, or that the laws of physics apply to all – to avoid the need to question the way they do things'.[11] Similarly, Prescod-Weinstein argues that what she calls white empiricism has come to 'dominate empirical discourse in physics because whiteness powerfully shapes the predominant arbiters of who is a valid observer of physical and social phenomena'.[12]

We see similar claims in other science fields. For example, the Quality Assurance Agency provides guidance for all UK universities. In its 2022 maths guidance, it has argued that the UK-wide Mathematics, Statistics and Operational Research (MSOR) 'curriculum should present a multicultural and decolonised view' that is 'informed by the student voice'. Similarly, the values of 'EDI should permeate the curriculum and every aspect of the learning experience to ensure the diverse nature of society in all its forms is evident'. Providers 'should reflect on their curricula and processes to ensure that no group is disadvantaged or othered; for example, decolonising the curriculum can involve explicit reflection on the history of MSOR knowledge generation, as well as reflecting on how delivery or admission practices might adversely impact on certain subgroups within the student cohort. EDI aspects of student engagement and achievement should be monitored and actions formed to ensure equity.'[13] This is a form of magical thinking whereby the beliefs (or rather the author's identity) somehow transmogrify that which is being examined and is rooted in the social constructivism we discussed above.

The laws of physics or maths exist independently of the scientist's identity. Our knowledge of those laws is fallible and relative but, given the mind independence of the phenomenon our knowledge gradually uncovers, we can rationally adjudicate between different interpretations to ascertain veracity and optimal explanations that are, in turn, superseded as learning progresses.

A key problem that Olúfẹ́mi Táíwò identifies is that this decolonial critique fully embraces 'the racialisation of consciousness', where modernity and science are seen as 'white' and therefore, in some intrinsic way anti-black.[14] In this, Africans or, more broadly, the agency of non-European cultures are portrayed as either victims or resisters against modernity itself 'rather than critical appropriators of it'.[15] Táíwò argues that this 'absolutisation of European colonialism' turns Africans into 'permanent subalterns in their history'. Instead, he says that we need to take African agency and the histories of non-European states and civilisations seriously, and not as mere objects of European perfidiousness without their own agency, interests and accounts. Through the castigation of modernity or the broader scientific Enlightenment as racially tainted, a 'hermeneutics of suspicion' is introduced, which undermines the capacity for democratic dialogue. Life becomes an endless struggle that pits people against one another based on identity.[16]

This also has implications for the nature of African governance today. It is extremely common to link problems in contemporary Africa to colonialism. For example, Olivia Rutazibwa argues that it is only 'through sustained colonial amnesia in knowledge production in [Western] society that the ills in the global South are systematically and almost exclusively attributed to the now and the local (over there)'. Instead, she claims that any analysis of the failure of African governance, lack of development and state capacity must 'foreground the transatlantic slave trade and the colonial encounter as the sites from which any thinking about development-related issues need to be addressed'.[17]

It is undeniable that the legacy of colonialism continues to reverberate in modern Africa. However, there is danger in always foregrounding colonialism. What role does African post-colonial agency and responsibility have in accounting for the lack of capacity in some African states and, more importantly, are African post-colonial elites not using the 'blame the West' narrative to cover for their own corruption? Aside from the tragedy of underdevelopment, this narrative lessens accountability. To give an example: in Nigeria, Africa's most populous nation, nearly $600 billion has been stolen by post-colonial Nigerian elites.[18] James Ibori, a former governor of Nigeria's Delta State, served a prison sentence in Britain for his role in plundering $79m from the public purse funds. His lawyers stymied the repatriation of the money from his British bank accounts. Regardless, Ifeanyi Okowa, the Delta State's governor argued that Ibori was 'a true patriot' and praised him for his 'uncompromising posture on . . . good governance'.[19] Adekoya argues that this reinforces an 'incredibly paternalistic and patronising attitude to Africans, painting them as helpless children who, even when they steal from their people, probably do it because the white man has told them to. All this only serves to downplay the role of corrupt African leaders in impoverishing their people.'[20]

This is perhaps becoming more urgent, with the 'blame the West' narrative having significant implications in giving African rulers a smokescreen to cover their own greed. A 2021 survey of citizens in 34 African countries showed that a clear majority feel that corruption was worsening, with 71% fearing retaliation if they dared to report problems.[21] Interestingly, and again counter-intuitively, a clear majority of Africans aged 18–24 believes that the impact their country's former colonial powers has on their education systems is positive, and a clear majority argues that trade relations with former colonial powers is having a positive impact. The same major survey even showed that 47% think the former colonial power's impact on their country's culture is positive.[22] In short, there is a significant disconnect between what Africans think and what largely Western-educated decolonial activists claim. To the extent that African political agency is not given the respect it deserves, we will continue to see a lack of accountability and a degradation of African governance through theft and corruption.

This is further reinforced given China's growing power and presence in Africa. Unlike Western aid, China's development finance loans to Africa, most of which are near market rates, have exploded in the last two decades. Between 2000 and 2020 the Chinese state lent $160bn to African governments, almost two-thirds of which was purely for infrastructure. Between 2007 and 2020, Chinese loans for infrastructure for sub-Saharan Africa were 2.5 times as much as for all other bilateral institutions combined.[23] This has led many analysts to argue that China is using its debt leverage over poorer African nations to extract raw materials and gain a strategic foothold across the continent. Some have even gone so far as to label this a new form of Chinese colonialism.[24] This is interesting on various levels, not least the history of China's role in African slavery.

For example, from the ninth century on, African slaves were common in the households of Arab merchants residing in Chinese port cities such as Guangzhou, which housed a significant Arab community.[25] This led to an increasing number of wealthy Chinese demanding such slaves in large numbers, and the development of a supply line beginning from

East Africa, traversing the Indian Ocean, stopping in India and finally crossing the Malaccan Straits to reach the port cities of China.[26] Most African slaves were used for hard labour. In his seminal book, Wyatt argues that the Chinese system of enslavement of Africans was as oppressive and cruel as slavery in the nineteenth-century United States.[27]

Lim concludes that the original sin of slavery is not unique to a specific 'culture or historical epoch but is an unfortunate constant in every human civilisation. What is different is how modern nations have come to terms with the legacy of slavery. In the West, this history is part of the school curriculum. It is portrayed in books, films and TV series.' He continues that, in contrast, the history of African slavery in China is largely unknown. It is not taught in schools or portrayed in 'popular culture and the link to anti-black racism is not acknowledged. In effect, the evidence of African slaves has been scrubbed from the Chinese collective memory and replaced with the regime's sanitised version of history. Outside China, we can still challenge this account. This makes it especially important to broaden discussions of historical slavery beyond the trans-atlantic slave trade to include the far older Indo-Pacific route as well.'[28]

This historical myopia on the part of the decolonial critique reflects an inward-looking form of Eurocentric narcissism. In *The Tyranny of Guilt: An Essay on Western Masochism*, Bruckner argues that the West has a deeply ingrained sense of guilt that feeds a paternalistic need to endlessly atone 'for what we have inflicted on other parts of humanity'. He continues: how 'can we fail to see that this leads us to live off self-denunciation while taking a strange pride in being the worst? Self-denigration is all too often a form of indirect self-glorification.' As such, the decolonial critique places Europe centre stage yet again, while also erasing the agency, complex histories, and ways in which non-Western states and civilisations have shaped history.[29]

Edward Said even noted this omission himself. In his post-colonial critique of Western Orientalism, he stated that there 'are several empires that I do not discuss: the Austro-Hungarian, the Russian, the Ottoman, and the Spanish and Portuguese'. These imperial states governed the lives of hundreds of millions of subjects, were engaged in extra-territorial domination and, especially in the case of the Ottoman Empire, were not only involved in slavery but were intimately bound up with European state formation. As we see below, we can add many more to Said's list.

Why would Said omit these from his wide-ranging critique of culture and imperialism? He says that because of the role of literature in the Anglophone West, coupled with the fact he 'feels at home' both in Western countries and is from the Occupied Palestinian territories, he can thus 'live on both sides' and therefore does not need to examine non-European empires.[30] As Puri notes, this selectivity on the part of Said 'is inadequate for our age of greater competition between a rich variety of countries'. He continues that solely focusing on 'western European imperialism and American neo-imperialism with dedicated fury is not representative of the full range of imperial legacies that still matter'. Were 'Europe's colonial empires in a different category of insidiousness from the Chinese, Russian, Ottoman and others? . . . The West did not have a monopoly over empire, since empires emerged on all continents for thousands of years.'[31]

Said's selectivity indicates a broader historical myopia on the part of the decolonisation and progressive movement that draws from a narrative of Western villainy versus non-Western saintliness. Beyond being patronisingly simplistic, it is vital that we examine rationally the rich history of the non-Western world in order to help restore some balance and see non-Western cultures and histories as having as much agency as our own, warts and all. In the next section, I examine some of these histories to show just how prevalent and important these are to the modern world.

## History reclaimed

As we have seen in previous chapters, the transatlantic slave trade plays a huge part in the decolonial critique of Western civilisation. Kehinde Andrews, arguably one of the UK's leading critical race theorists, captures the sentiment well when he argues that the West is founded on 'genocide, slavery and colonialism' and its wealth today is directly traceable to that terrible trade in human souls. The new 'anti-racism' explicitly utilises this history in its moral critique of the UK as anti-racism 'cannot be framed as a diversity project without understanding the colonial structures of racial injustice that created the slave trade'.[32]

Britain's role in the slave trade continues to impact politics hugely in the UK today. As we have seen, following the rise of the Black Lives Matter movement, the UK has been swept up in a wave of iconoclasm, which has seen statues toppled and British institutions becoming hyper-aware of the issues of racism and Britain's role in the slave trade. In a sense, this 'original sin' is used to generate forms of often radical political and cultural transformation across institutions in the Anglophone West. The atonement for this history is thus the ethical keystone that helps drive the broader changes being wrought on British society.

The transatlantic slave trade operated from the sixteenth to the nineteenth centuries and transported between ten and twelve million Africans. It relied on European slavers trading commodities such as wine, guns and textiles with African slave kingdoms, shipping slaves from Africa to the Americas and then commodities such as sugar and coffee back to Europe; a so-called triangular trade. From 1640 Britain was one of the predominant slave trading nations until the Abolition of the Slave Trade act was passed in 1807. The act stated that all 'manner of dealing and reading in the purchase, sale, barter, or transfer of slaves or of persons intending to be sold, transferred, used, or dealt with as slaves, practised or carried in, at, or from any part of the coast or countries of Africa shall be abolished, prohibited and declared to be unlawful'.

Following the law, it became illegal to purchase enslaved people directly from Africa, thus outlawing the slave trade. Despite the passing of the 1807 act, slave owners and other powerful interests sought to resist this, and slavery as an institution remained legal in the British Caribbean and other parts of the British Empire; many slave owners were unwilling to give up their enslaved labour force without compensation. As a result, there was significant resistance to the abolition of slavery, and it took many years of campaigning by abolitionists and other advocates for the abolition of slavery to build support for the Slavery Abolition Act. The condition of slavery remained legal in the British Caribbean until 1834, when the Slavery Abolition Act 1833 finally came into force.[33]

It is important to recognise this history, which is why it is taught in most schools. We should remain cognisant of the horror and human suffering of the transatlantic slave trade. However, not only has slavery been ubiquitous throughout human history, but so have non-European empires, colonialism, and great power competition. Indeed, the dominant norm throughout most of human history has been territorial acquisition through domination, conflict and war. The idea that a weaker foe's claims to land should be respected out of charity or an amorphous set of rights has, as Russia's 2022 invasion of Ukraine reminds us, simply not been the norm for most of humanity's history.

## Slavery in human history

Britain and the West do not have a monopoly on slavery. Indeed, like war and conflict, slavery has been the norm throughout human history and its ending, in the West at least, is more of an historical anomaly. Even today, a 2021 United Nations report concluded that an 'estimated 40.3 million people are in modern slavery, including 24.9 in forced labour and 15.4 million in forced marriage'. Shockingly, one in four victims of modern slavery are children.[34]

Of contemporary slavery, India has the largest slave popu-lation today, standing at just under eight million. Its large population partially explains this, but also because 'all forms of modern slavery exist in India, including forced child labor, forced marriage, commercial sexual exploitation, bonded labor, and forced recruitment into armed groups'.[35] This should also be seen within the broader system of India's caste system, with over 200 million Dalits, or so-called 'untouchables', facing regular violence and discrimination and India's elite Brahmin class controlling 60% of its wealth.[36] This discriminatory caste system survives internationally. For example, anti-caste campaigners in the UK are calling for caste discrimination leg-islation and 'estimate there are up to half a million Dalits in the UK who could be at risk of caste prejudice'.[37]

Similarly, Anti-Slavery International's report outlined the continued modern-day prevalence of descent-based slavery, whereby people are born into slavery because their ancestors were captured into slavery. They conclude that this 'form of slavery can still be found across the Sahel belt of Africa, including Mauritania, Niger, Mali, Chad and Sudan'. And many 'other African societies also have a traditional hierarchy where people are known to be the descendants of slaves or slave-owners'.[38]

Beyond the tragedy of modern-day slavery, covered above to put into perspective just how common this trade in human souls sadly still is, it also highlights the crucial question of how has slavery traditionally been ended, given its historical ubiquity right up to the present day?

## What ends slavery?

In the case of Britain, it was a combination of slave revolts, most notably in Haiti, and the rise of the domestic abolitionist movement in Britain itself.[39] As such, in the final instance, abolition was not forced onto Britain by a superior military power, but was a choice, whose domestic consensus was built by the tireless work of the abolitionist movement, which drew on both Christian and Enlightenment thinking as to the universal humanity and equality of all people.

Britain ended the slave trade first in its colonies, and then the British Royal Navy took on a new global mission to rid the world forcibly of slavery. While still at war with France in the Napoleonic wars, two anti-slavery warships were sent to police African waters. In 1808, the West Africa Squadron was formed, whose sole mission was to suppress the Atlantic slave trade, which was still conducted mainly by Portugal and Spain. When the Napoleonic Wars ended, Viscount Castlereagh ensured that a declaration against slavery appeared in the text of the Congress of Vienna, which committed its signatories to the eventual abolition of the trade. France did so in 1814, and Spain agreed in 1817 to cease its slaving North of the equator. Despite this, the French repeatedly refused to allow the Royal Navy to stop suspected French slavers.

As Black concludes, the '1845 Slave Trade Act authorised the navy to treat suspected slave ships as pirates, leading to the capture of nearly 400 ships within five years'. He continues that by the end of the '1840s, there were 35 anti-slaving patrol ships off West Africa. The slave trade to Brazil, the largest market in the southern hemisphere, was ended by the Royal

Navy.'[40] Brazil's huge trade in slaves was ended when the Royal Navy destroyed their slaving fleet.

The Royal Navy lost 17,000 men in its commitment to ending slavery off the West coast of Africa. By 1860, the Royal Navy's West Africa Squadron had seized approximately 1,600 ships involved in slavery and freed 150,000 Africans aboard those vessels.[41] Aside from the use of the Royal Navy, the effort was also political and consular, with pressure placed on West African rulers, the Ottoman Empire and on Arab rulers in Zanzibar and Sudan to desist from slave trading. This often included the transfers of huge sums to pay them off from their participation in the slave trade. British consular officials also worked against it, often clandestinely, in Egypt, North Africa and the Caribbean.[42]

The Royal Navy then moved its attention to the Indian Ocean to help suppress the long-standing Arab trade in African slaves to the Middle East. Indeed, once the Atlantic slave trade was abolished, the much longer-standing Eastern trade simply expanded, with the West's efforts in ending the trade tragically offset by the expansion of the Eastern trade. Also noteworthy was the fact that unlike 'the Atlantic slave traders, Muslims enslaved people from many cultures as well as Africa. Other sources included the Balkans, Central Asia and Mediterranean Europe'.[43]

## Slavery in Africa

The Afro-Omani ivory and slave trader, Tippu Tip, is popularly considered to be one of history's most prominent slavers, and ran an extensive and highly stratified trading system in East Africa, with slaves used to transport ivory, and was responsible for supplying much of the world with black slaves.[44] By 1895, Tip controlled seven huge plantations in Zanzibar, with an estimated 10,000 slaves.[45] Tippu Tip stood at the apex of an

extensive system of slavery: 'Islamic traders from Zanzibar
and the east coast saw themselves as the political and social
overlords' and, although subordinate to 'Tippu Tip, each
individual was in his own right a coloniser and a planter of
the first order', with indigenous African slaves 'the means of
realising that status'.[46] Laura Fair argued that '[s]laves, and
the profit derived from both their sale and their labor, were
at the very heart of Zanzibar's transformation from a small
and relatively unimportant Swahili town to the centre of a
vast trading empire stretching from central Africa to halfway
around the world.'[47] In 1890, the British government signed a
treaty with the Zanzibari royal family to end the slave trade in
their territories. This treaty, along with the efforts of abolitionist groups, contributed to the eventual abolition of slavery in
Zanzibar. However, Tip's legacy remained with clear distinc-
tions 'between slaves and the free, urbanites and rural dwellers,
mainlanders and islanders and Arab and African. Divisions
that are still apparent in the pre- and post-revolution politics
of Tanzania.'[48]

The involvement of the Islamic world in African slavery
is long-standing and was not just confined to East Africa.
Indeed, the Sokoto Caliphate was a West African Empire that
was later incorporated into northern Nigeria. Founded by the
Islamic scholar and political leader Usman dan Fodio after
he conquered the Hausa people, it remained one of the largest empires in Africa throughout the nineteenth century. It
was located in what is now modern-day Nigeria and covered
an area that included parts of present-day Niger, Chad and
Cameroon. The caliphate was known for its strict adherence to
Islamic law and its centralised government, which was based
on the Islamic legal system of sharia. The Sokoto Caliphate
was also an important centre of trade and education in West
Africa.

The Sokoto caliphate was 'one of the largest slave societies
in modern history'. Historians studying the Sokoto caliphate

argue that its slave population was 'certainly in excess of one million and perhaps more than 2.5 million people'.[49] Slavery was an important part of the economy and society of the Sokoto Caliphate. Enslaved people were used for a variety of purposes, including agricultural labour, domestic work, and as soldiers in the caliphal army. The slave trade was an important source of wealth for the caliphate, and slaves were traded both within West Africa and with other parts of the world. Most of its captives were usually children, taken 'in jihad from mainly non-Muslim communities, to serve as slaves. These slaves worked on farms or within households, they might be concubines and bear children for their owners; or they might be sold as children for export to North Africa in payment for the luxury imports the new elite wanted.'[50] As Bashir Salau argues, 'The nature of Sokoto caliphate plantations tells us that slaves were typically acquired through acts of violence and as such were usually "outsiders" stripped of their social identity.' This status 'allowed masters to buy and sell them, thereby placing them into the category of property'.[51] It should also be noted that it is often bizarrely asserted that Islamic slavery was more benign relative to European slavery. Despite the morally dubious nature of this assertion, Azumah notes that in the handful of cases where black slaves rose to positions of prominence, this could only be obtained via castration under the 'gelder's knife' and as a result of sex slavery. He notes that 'most if not all other persons of black descent who attained some kind of fame in the Muslim world (mainly in poetry and music) were almost always the offspring of concubines'.[52]

Similarly, the Barbary slave trade (so-called because it operated from the Barbary Coast of North Africa) was central to the white slave trade. It raided so deep into Europe that there are accounts of Barbary slavers operating off the coast of Iceland in 1627. Estimates vary, but at its height the Barbary states of Tunis, Algiers and Tripoli alone enslaved over a million Europeans between the sixteenth century and the middle of the eighteenth century.[53] Indeed, in the 1620s, more British subjects lived as slaves in Islamic North Africa than as freemen in the colonies of North America.[54] The Barbary slavers mainly raided Ireland and the South West of England. One raid on a Cornish village in 1645 saw 240 men, women and children taken off into slavery. Invariably the men were forced into a brutal system of galley slavery, and the women taken as sex slaves within the Barbary's seraglio (harem) system.[55] The raids became so intense that England's fishing industry became paralysed (for fear of seaborne capture). In response, Oliver Cromwell ordered a naval bombardment of Lundy Island to dislodge a Barbary stronghold.[56]

The Barbary white slave trade was significantly constrained when the United States launched two naval wars in the early 1800s to end the trade and was only finally suppressed with the French conquest of Algeria in 1830.[57] The trade was eventually ended due to a combination of factors, including military action by European powers, the abolition of the slave trade by the Ottoman Empire, and the growing power of the European colonial empires in Africa. Its ending also fortuitously contributed to the growing movement against slavery in the United States. Leading abolitionists like Charles Sumner 'found a universal theme from the 1815–16 victory over slavery in Islamic North Africa. As Sumner put it, "Slavery in all its forms, even under the mildest influences, is a wrong and a curse."'[58]

Importantly, it should also be noted that the Barbary states and transatlantic slavers did not 'create' the slave trade. Rather, they worked through an already long-established slave system that pre-dated European contact with the African continent. As already noted, historically, most slaves are taken in the context of war victory and conquest. The same is true throughout Africa pre-European contact. As Abdulazizi Lodhi notes, when 'it came to exports, tribal Africans were the main actors. In many African societies there were no prisons, so people who were captured were sold'.[59]

On the external trade, Lovejoy concludes that 24 million slaves were exported from sub-Saharan Africa in the eleven centuries from 800 to 1900. The Atlantic slave trade accounted for nearly 13 million or a little over half of this total. The Islamic slave trade to Muslim states in the Middle East, North Africa, Europe and Asia took the rest at over 11 million.[60] However, on a longer time scale and factoring in the trade across the Sahara, some estimates argue the Arab slave trade trafficked up to 17 million (9 million across Sahara, 8 million by sea).[61]

Thornton argues that intra-African slavery 'was already pre-figured by the history of social stratification, war, and captivity in Africa, both before the trans-Atlantic slave trade started, and during the time of the slave trade – before enslaved Africans entered European ships'. He continues that 'European merchants had little or no involvement in the first part of the slaves' journey; that portion was in Africa and was generally the work of African rulers, merchants, and sometimes lawless figures like bandits.' As such, 'understanding the larger African past is as essential to understanding slavery and the slave trade as knowing the history of Europe or the Americas'.[62]

The commercial records show this quite clearly. Thornton argues that the records of the Dutch West India Company, formed in 1621, provide the fullest accounts of slave exports. Its records exceed 100,000 pages, and there is 'scarcely any mention of direct enslavement of Africans', as European merchants 'acquired their slaves by purchase from African buyers, usually with the active participation of African states, both as taxing agencies and in their own right as commercial sellers'.[63] As such, the delivery of enslaved Africans to Europeans was an African business managed by African commercial and political elites. Many of the descendants of these elites, enriched at the expense of fellow Africans, continue to rule many African states today. Indeed, Perbi notes that there 'were two dimensions to slavery and the slave trade in pre-colonial Africa, an external and internal dimension. The external dimension involved trade across the Sahara, the Mediterranean, the Red Sea, the Arabic and Indian ocean worlds.' The internal dimension was primarily based on the use of slaves for agriculture.[64]

Most notable of the African slave states was the Kingdom of Dahomey in West Africa.[65] It existed from 1600 until 1904. The Kingdom of Dahomey was an African kingdom located in what is now modern-day Benin. The kingdom was known for its military might and its reliance on slavery as a key part of its economy. Dahomey was ruled by a series of kings, the most notable of whom was King Ghezo, who ruled from 1818 to 1858. During his reign, King Ghezo oversaw the expansion of the Dahomey kingdom and increased its wealth through the capture and sale of slaves. The kingdom's slave trade was primarily focused on the Yoruba Empire of Oyo, which was conquered by Dahomey and became a major source of slaves for the kingdom. Many of these slaves were put to work on the royal plantations, while others were sold to European slave traders. Despite its reputation as a slave state, the Kingdom of Dahomey also had a complex and highly developed system of government, including a well-trained army and a sophisticated bureaucracy.

An annual festival was held in honour of the kingdom's founding ancestors and was a display of Dahomean culture and traditions. It was an important event in Dahomean society and was attended by people from all walks of life, including the king, nobles and commoners.

During the festival, various ceremonies and rituals were performed, including music, dancing, and the re-enactment of historical events.[66] The festival also featured the public sacrifice of slaves. As many as 4,000 were executed in 1727 alone as part of the festival celebrations. The 'Customs of Dahomey' festival was eventually abolished in the late nineteenth century due to pressure from European colonial powers and the efforts of abolitionist groups. Dahomey's fortunes in conquest and slavery were only ended with the cessation of slave exports to Brazil and other efforts by the British to suppress the Kingdom's slaving. This met stiff resistance, and it was not until 1851 that a British naval blockade of Dahomey saw its terrible trade in human souls finally end.[67] Bizarrely, Dahomey, responsible for the mass murder of black slaves, was celebrated in a Hollywood blockbuster called *The Woman King* in 2022.

## Did slavery make Britain rich?

This distressing history of slavery, which we have examined above, shows that slavery has been common across all human civilisations as an institution. The historical narrative that we have examined in previous chapters seeks to attribute responsibility and guilt to the UK in the present day. It is based on the moral power of what is a partial account of transatlantic slavery, which academic theorists of the decolonisation movement and their university enablers use to castigate 'whiteness' and the seemingly collective racial guilt of all white people today. This narrative becomes far harder to sustain when considering the historical record.

The decolonisation movement's invocation of history is both simplistic and overly Eurocentric. It erases the complex (and often brutal) history of non-European peoples, civilisations and states. It reproduces a simplistic binary of European evil vs non-European good, when the record is not only far more mixed, but the British were active anti-slavers following abolition across Africa and the wider global South. Intra-African slavery, most often through war and conquest, was the norm, and long pre-dated the transatlantic slave trade.

This intra-African slave trade, run by various African kingdoms, existed alongside the well-established Islamic slave trade too. Most forms of organised global slavery were brought to an end by the combination of slave revolts that raised the costs of its gruesome trade and, in the context of the Atlantic slave trade, the decisive military intervention of the British. This is not discussed here to diminish the horror of the transatlantic slave trade or to engage in a form of historical 'whataboutery' but to put into historical perspective some of the key events, facts and histories that inform present-day debates around decolonisation, British institutional 'guilt' and what this means for British identity.

However, as we saw in previous chapters, the charge is not just that Britain and the West in general participated in the slave trade, but that the trade created a legacy of unequal and unjust economic enrichment on the part of Britain. As we saw in previous chapters, the new history of capitalism thesis states that 'industrial capitalism and the Great Divergence' between the West and the global South 'emerged from the violent cauldron of slavery, colonialism, and the expropriation of land'. It helps explain current disparities and alleged racism in the present day.[68] It is argued that the 'backs and souls of enslaved people built Britain – the backs of those who toiled in cotton fields and plantations in British colonies, and the souls of those who did not survive the journey'.[69] As such, today's UK and, by extension, the white majority is collectively guilty and 'owes' both a moral and financial debt to the descendants of the victims of the transatlantic slave trade. Indeed, there is an active ongoing campaign for reparations.[70]

How accurate is this charge? It is undeniable that small groups of individuals in Great Britain, often drawn from the aristocracy and economic and political elites often personally benefited enormously from slavery.[71] Colston, whose statue was thrown in the River Avon by BLM protesters in 2020 is but one example. The Centre for the Study of the Legacies of British Slavery has a fascinating database on individuals and families directly benefiting from the transatlantic slave trade.[72] The Slavery Abolition Act of 1833 provided £20 million to compensate 3,000 slave proprietors. Its distribution was overseen by the Slave Compensation Commission and made by the UK National Debt Office.[73] At the time, this represented 40% of the Treasury's annual spending budget. This was a massive sum, with one of the most significant pay-outs going to John Gladstone, the father of nineteenth-century prime minister William Gladstone, who got £106,769 (modern equivalent £83m) for the slaves he owned across nine plantations.[74] Morally repugnant as this is to us in the modern day, it was designed to ease the passage of abolition by placating the powerful and politically entrenched interests of those who stood to lose from its dissolution. It was done to expedite the ending of the institution of slavery within the British Empire.

While huge for a small number of individuals, however, the profits and associated industries were not big enough to change the economic fortunes of Britain as a whole.[75] As Mokyr argues, the development of British capitalism and the Industrial Revolution is only tangentially linked to slavery. He goes on to say that it is 'hard to see exactly how the imperial policies, which protected British merchants doing business overseas, could have had much impact on the Industrial Revolution beyond, perhaps, assuring favourable treatment in some markets'. In short, the British Empire's foreign policy conveyed a slight advantage. After all, Britain lost the United States, which was 'one of its richest colonies during the early stages of the Industrial Revolution and yet, after 1783, commercial relations with the young United States were none the worse for wear until complications in Europe drove the two apart again'. Concerning West India, slavery as an institution was 'important to Britain as a source of products that could not be produced locally' given the climate, most notably sugar. However, and in no way diminishing the brutality of Caribbean slavery, in its absence, Mokyr argues that 'Britain would have had to drink bitter tea, but it still would have had an Industrial Revolution, if perhaps at a marginally slower pace.'[76]

As Eltis and Engerman have shown, the slave trade only constituted a small portion of British overseas commerce. In 1792, the most significant year, 204 vessels of an aggregate 38,099 tonnes left British ports. However, in the same year, there were 14,334 ships registered in Britain, grossing 1.44 million tons. So, only 1.5% of British ships and 3% of tonnage were involved in the slave trade. They continue that if 'economic activity on so modest a scale could contribute significantly to industriali-sation, then we might expect Europe's first industrial economy to have been Portugal, not Britain. Though Portugal had less than one-third the population of Britain in the late eighteenth century, and a total national income, which was no doubt still lesser, the country's nationals nevertheless managed to carry nearly two-thirds again as many slaves across the Atlantic than did the British over the course of the slave-trade era.'[77]

Moreover, the logic of capitalism itself would suggest that if sugar, the primary commodity produced by slaves on the major Caribbean islands, yielded a massively higher return on investment, capitalists would shift their assets into the sugar industry during this period. However, sugar 'was just one of hundreds of industries in a complex economy; and, while sugar was one of the larger industries, its linkages with the rest of the economy and its role as an "engine" of economic growth compare poorly with textiles, coal, iron ore, and those British agricultural activities which provided significant inputs to industry'.[78] In short, the sugar industry was equivalent to barley and hops and brewing in terms of economic outputs. While some individuals made huge profits on a disgusting trade to produce a commodity popular with the rich, it was not central to the Industrial Revolution. Would anybody argue that Britain's Industrial Revolution would never have hap-pened without beer?

Indeed, one analysis concludes that the possession of the British West Indies had the effect of retarding the growth of Great Britain's economy. The 'income of Englishmen would have been at least £500,000 higher in the absence of the West Indies from the Empire'.[79] If slavery were the engine of Great

Britain's wealth, why are other societies that also practised slavery not as wealthy?

The British Empire required steam and steel ships after the Industrial Revolution had already begun. Indeed, leading economic historians have concluded that the principal points of the 'Great Divergence' in GDP between (primarily northern) Europe and the Mediterranean area occurred as a result of the structural effects of the Black Death in 1348 and the opening of new trade routes around 1500. These events combined with state capacity and the enforcement of property rights to enhance economic growth long pre-dated formal colonisation and the Transatlantic slave trade.[80]

As such, the slave trade likely heightened inequality in Britain itself, between a small elite who got ever more affluent and the great mass of the British population that lived in poverty. The trend of rising GDP in Great Britain, while influenced by a range of variables, long pre-dated formal colonisation and the slave trade. There are strong arguments that the diversion of capital to service the economic and foreign-policy interests of this already wealthy class added to this immiseration. On the compensation to slave owners alone, think how that huge sum could have transformed the lives of millions of impoverished British citizens who had no say whatsoever on slavery, imperial policy or compensation to economic and political elites in Britain at that time.

## The life of ordinary people in the UK during the time of slavery

It is crucial that we also examine the life of ordinary people in Britain at the time of slavery and after its abolition. As we have seen, the broader progressive identity politics and decolonisation movement makes an explicitly generalised critique of the collective racial guilt of white people ('whiteness') and British

institutions that need to 'decolonise' to atone for historical
sins. How accurate is this theory of collective racial responsibility and white privilege?

First, it should be noted that universal suffrage did not exist
in Britain until 1928. The Representation of the People Act of
1918 extended suffrage by abolishing men's property qualifications and enfranchising women over thirty who met minimum
property qualifications. All women, regardless of property
qualifications, were given the right to vote in 1928. In early
nineteenth-century Britain practically nobody had the right to
vote. A survey conducted in 1780 showed that the electorate in
England and Wales consisted of 214,000 people; less than 3%
of the total population of approximately eight million at the
time.

In Scotland, 4,500 men (out of a population of more than
2.6 million) were entitled to vote in parliamentary elections.[81]
As such, and reflecting what we explored above, Britain was
not a democracy, but was in fact controlled by a tiny ruling
class. The British population did not 'vote' for the Empire or
transatlantic slavery – they had no say whatsoever. Indeed,
even on a much smaller level, many of the sailors within the
Royal Navy were effectively violently kidnapped into it with
the practice known as impressment, by what became known
colloquially as the Press Gang. Press gangs used physical force
and violence to kidnap men to serve on the Navy's ships and
was so widespread that in its declaration of war against the
British in 1812, the US government cited, in part, the Navy's
use of Impressment as a cause of the war, when it kidnapped
over 15,000 US sailors to bolster the numbers during their
Napoleonic Wars with France.[82]

Second, beyond the political configuration of Great Britain,
the conditions for most of the British population in the 1800s
and beyond were often nasty, brutish and short. Life expectancy in 1841 for the average man was a mere forty years.[83]
Child labour was common. In 1838, following thunderstorms,

a stream overflowed into a ventilation shaft of the Huskar mining Colliery in Silkstone. Eleven girls aged from eight to sixteen and fifteen boys between nine and twelve years of age died. Following media coverage in London, an enquiry was held by Lord Ashley. His findings contain harrowing details. Eight-year-old Sarah Gooder was a trapper, a job that often went to the youngest in mine families and whose job would be to sit in total darkness, often for up to twelve hours, and to open wooden trap doors to allow fresh air into the deep mines. Bravely she states that the job 'does not tire me, but I have to trap without a light and I'm scared. I go at four and sometimes half past three in the morning and come out at five and half past (in the afternoon)'.[84] Often women would also work deep in the mines. Betty Wardle, who had worked in the mines since the age of six, told the enquiry that 'I had a child born in the pits, and I brought it up the pit-shaft in my skirt.' The last chimney sweep 'climbing boy' died in 1875. George Brewster was only eleven years old when he became trapped in a former Victorian asylum in Fulbourn, Cambridgeshire. Brewster's mother died when he was very young, and in what was a common practice for thousands of children in Victorian England, was sold by his impoverished family into an 'apprenticeship'.[85]

In the East End slums of Victorian London (where my own family come from), disease and poverty were rampant. The workhouses and poorhouses were used to contain 'surplus' populations and those too destitute to support themselves. Designed to be a place of last resort for people who were unable to support themselves, the conditions in the workhouses were often harsh and bleak. In what were often little more than prisons, inmates were fed gruel (a watery porridge) and sometimes spent up to sixteen hours a day on stone breaking or picking apart old rope. Modelled on Victorian prisons, workhouse inmates unrolled individual strands of rope to produce oakum used to caulk ships. It has been estimated that about 6.5% of the

British population may have been contained in workhouses at any given time.[86]

In short, the vast majority of the population in Britain at the time of transatlantic slavery, and after its ending, were desperately poor, and lived in conditions where disease, hunger and poverty were rampant, and the vast majority were dead at forty years old. Britain was not a democracy, and nobody voted for slavery or the Empire. It was a choice made by the ruling classes of Great Britain. As we have examined above, the maintenance of that Empire came a great cost to the largely destitute population of the UK, including the compensation paid to the slave owners. Slavery, colonisation, and imperial domination do not belong to any state, civilisation or race of people, and its manifestation has been the norm throughout human history.

The abolitionist movement in Britain, which sought to end the transatlantic slave trade and slavery in the British Empire, was supported by a diverse group of people from various social classes; most notably ordinary people, including factory workers and artisans, who saw slavery as an injustice and were motivated to speak out against it. One of the key ways in which working-class people supported the abolitionist movement was by participating in boycotts of slave-produced goods, such as sugar and tobacco. These boycotts were organised by groups like the Society for the Abolition of the Slave Trade and the Association for Promoting the Abolition of Slavery and were designed to put economic pressure on slave-holding countries and industries. Working-class people also participated in protests and petition campaigns and contributed money to support the cause.

This puts the decolonisation movement, and the broader progressive movement into perspective. The invocation of whiteness and its associated concepts such as white privilege is factually inaccurate and morally repugnant. It blames all white people, the vast majority of whom are descendants of those who lived desperately poor lives, for the actions and choices of a tiny aristocracy and ruling class, many of whom continue to enjoy astonishing privileges today. Indeed, our most elite institutions often take the privately educated children of these same elites, who often champion the decolonial critique that conveniently elides their socio-economic privileges with an undifferentiated white 'other'. When called to do so, and motivated by the moral repugnance of slavery, those same ordinary people, whose descendants are now castigated today, acted to help end slavery as part of a wider movement for abolition.

Many aspects of the progressive culture war are part of a larger class war. The fact that these ideas now enjoy such wide purchase among those who now run British institutions, especially our universities, which are supposed to be custodians of social mobility, is a puzzle examined in the next chapter. How did identity politics and broader wokery become so prevalent? Where did it come from and why does it enjoy such cultural and political power today? That is the subject of our next chapter.

# 5

# Accounting for 'wokery'

I opened this book with a puzzle. Opinion poll after opinion poll and metric after metric show that the UK is now one of the least racist countries in the world. The preceding chapters show that many ethnic minorities do better in many areas than the white majority: from educational outcomes to earnings and life expectancy. This is a story of immigrant and integration success.

Even among the UK's diverse population, the emphasis on racial grievance and a view of Britain as a malign influence on world history does not chime well. For example, one of the most extensive studies on race in the UK tracked 40,000 households, 10,000 of which were ethnic minority individuals polled for their opinions. It found that ethnic minorities in Britain identify more strongly with 'Britishness' than their white counterparts.[1] The think tank British Future, which specialises in identity, immigration and race, came to a similar conclusion. Asians in Britain, it stated, 'have the strongest sense of British belonging, with 70% saying they belong strongly, compared to 66% of white Britons'. Of the British population, Muslims are the most likely of the various groups to consider themselves British, with Pakistani Muslims most closely identifying as British.[2]

Despite this, the dominant elite cultural narrative views the UK as irredeemably racist. As we have seen, its history is denigrated as a litany of exploitation, and its institutions are undergoing a profound transformation to address these alleged sins: decolonisation. I have shown how this is operating in, arguably, some of our most important institutions responsible for shaping the minds of millions of young people and, thus, the future of the country: British universities.

Rather than being a sea of soft progressivism, our higher education institutions are said to be deeply compromised. In the words of Professor David Richardson, Chair of Universities UK's advisory group on racism, our higher education institutions are 'perpetuating systemic racism' and are 'institutionally racist'.[3] In addressing what is a manufactured moral panic, supine university leaders, backed by activist students and staff, have openly endorsed theories that, less than ten years ago, were on the very edges of social-science and humanities research: from critical race theory to post-colonialism.

The key claim is an alleged negative disparity (degree gaps, staff gaps and so on) that is indicative of an underlying system of discrimination. This narrative is demonstrably false. One of the leading African American intellectuals, Thomas Sowell, has repeatedly debunked this narrative. Yet it remains stubbornly hardwired in progressive opinion both in the US and the UK, and forms one of the most critical intellectual ballasts of progressive politics. The equation is simplistic but effective and very conveniently always seems to require the political solutions offered by those claiming the existence of these hidden forms of systemic discrimination.[4]

Even if we accept this fallacious logic, study after study shows that white working-class young people, and men, remain the most disadvantaged at our universities. Suppose activists and technocrats took their claims seriously. In that case, the logical conclusion is that UK universities are structurally racist towards poor white people and sexist towards

men, given the considerable gender disparities across the UK
university student population. Moreover, given the claim
that education remains one of the leading drivers of equality
and social mobility, especially for those born without socio-
economic advantages, what does this say about the moral
failure of British universities? This is compounded when, even
if a young white working-class adult makes it onto campus,
they face a bureaucratic and intellectual environment that may
well endorse theories that single them out for their alleged
racial privileges and police their behaviour to drive out microaggressions or 'whiteness'.

It is undoubtable that some people are born with more privileges than others. Still, the Left-Liberal critique has shifted
from socio-economic class and educational background (the
lead determinants of future success) to one of identity as
indicative of privilege. Even second-hand clothes are coded
as evidence of white privilege, according to one of the many
compulsory courses now running through the UK university
system.[5] As such, in the purview of the modern social-justice
movement, there is no difference between a young white man
from Eton or one from a comprehensive in Hull: both are
said to have innate white privileges. However, the young man
from Eton will have the education and likely social confidence
to express the 'right' high-status opinions. In this way, his
incredible class privileges are collapsed into a lumpen 'white
mass' from which he is now distanced through his low-cost/
high-value progressive opinion signalling and thus elevated
moral status. Once again, the progressive culture war is part of
a broader class war.

This progressive assault shows little sign of abating as it
becomes ever more hardwired into mainstream politics and
thus hardens in our universities and across British institutions.
For example, the Labour party, the UK's main centre-Left party,
has enthusiastically championed the view that British society
is endemically racist, with white people enjoying a privileged

position due to their race. The 'idea that white privilege exists isn't extremist, it's a widely accepted fact', argued Labour's Bell Ribeiro-Addy.[6] As such, only Labour 'can be trusted to unlock the talent of black, Asian and minority ethnic people', argued former Labour leader Jeremy Corbyn. Keir Starmer, the current Labour leader, endorsed the UK BLM movement and stated it was a defining moment in British politics. Labour's shadow secretary for women and equalities, Marsha de Cordova argued that we 'cannot wait any longer to address the deep-rooted systemic racial inequalities across our society'.[7] Following a minute's silence to commemorate the killing of George Floyd, Starmer argued that he 'must not become just another name. His death must be a catalyst for change.'

In March 2021, the UK government's Commission on Race and Ethnic Disparities (CRED) released a detailed report on race relations and equality. At over 258 pages, it represents a landmark piece of research. It rejected the orthodoxies of the mainstream narrative that interprets ethnic disparities through the prism of systemic racism and institutional discrimination. The Commissioners state that they 'no longer see a Britain where the system is deliberately rigged against ethnic minorities' – arguing that racism is often used as a 'catch-all' explanation for the existence of ethnic disparities.[8]

Some adverse reactions to the report bordered on the hysterical. Even before the report was published. Dr Shola Mos-Shogbamimu, one of the UK's preeminent intersectional media interlocutors and granddaughter of the late Nigerian Monarch of Ogere-Remo, labelled the lead author, Dr Tony Sewell, a 'token black man' and stated that 'Britain is not a model of racial equality.'[9] Professor Priyamvada Gopal of Cambridge University questioned if he had a doctorate. When that was confirmed, she replied, 'Even Dr Goebbels had a research PhD.'[10] WonkHE, a leading resource for UK Vice Chancellors, described how by appearing to deny the veracity of 'anti-racist counternarratives' the mostly ethnic minority

commissioners of the report have created it to 'aspire to whiteness themselves'.[11]

Given the wholesale ideological adoption of identity politics by the Labour party, it was unsurprising that the Party's
reactions were similar. Without even having read the report,
the Labour leader Sir Keir Starmer condemned it as 'disap-
pointing', while Labour's Clive Lewis even sought to strike
parallels with the report's claims and the white supremacist
Ku Klux Klan (KKK). The report, 'rolls back decades of work
on challenging racial inequality and is an insult to everyone
who continues to experience institutional racism', argued the
MP, Bell Ribeiro-Addy.[12]

Starmer has now committed the Labour party to introducing a new Race Equality Act, which, he argued would 'tackle
structural racial inequality at source'.[13] Labour MP Marsha de
Cordova explained how the act would be shaped by people's
personal subjective feelings and anecdotes 'Labour will not
ignore the ambition of British people to build a better society for everyone. We have committed to introducing a Race
Equality Act shaped by lived experience.'[14] In helping drive this
forward, the Labour Party's 2022 'rule book' mentions black
and ethnic minority (BAME) representation 104 times, where
only two mentions are made to increasing working-class representation. Even then, class is subordinated to woke ideology.
While the party will seek to increase working-class representation, it will 'select more candidates who reflect the full diversity
of our society in terms of gender, race, sexual orientation and
disability'.[15]

In the previous chapters, we examined the historical and
theoretical claims made by the decolonial movement and how
this has been adopted within UK universities. I then showed
that these claims are deeply flawed. Against a very partial
reading of history, I instead drew out the role that Britain has
played in ending slavery in the context of its desperate poverty. Slavery, extra-territorial colonisation and conquest have

characterised human history, and Britain remains one of the handful of states that have not only voluntarily abrogated this foul system but sought to end it across the globe and thus liberate millions of souls from bondage.

This is not an ode to British morality or exceptionalism but rather a realist recognition of the nature of history and world politics. We should ask, why should a brief period in British history, which I have shown is itself complex, come to define its present and thus shape its future in such a profound way? We have yet to unpack what drives this movement across the Anglophone West. We do so now.

## Intersectional illiberalism

The ideas and ideologies I have examined in popular media are often referred to as 'woke' or 'wokery'. I have also invoked this term in previous chapters, but under that catch-all term are a range of ideas and debates.

Wokery draws on what is called 'intersectional' theory. As seen above, this theory foregrounds identity characteristics such as race, sexuality and gender and attempts to show that these come together as part of a kaleidoscope of intersecting oppressions. As Kimberlé Crenshaw, intersectionality's principal theorist, explains, it is 'about how certain aspects of who you are will increase your access to the good things or your exposure to the bad things in life'.[16] As such, politics becomes centred around identity issues with the critical goal of ensuring identity 'diversity' in positions of relative privilege and power to compensate for what are said to be historically oppressed groups.

All societies have deeper norms and values that help govern social organisation. Worryingly, intersectionality shifts what we might call the apex value that has guided the UK and the West more generally in the increasingly meritocratic post-war period. Rather than ability or merit (which, as we have seen, are often denounced as parts of a 'white supremacy culture'), the new apex value is becoming 'diversity' in and of itself. This is deeply problematic.

First, diversity has historically been little more than one of many by-products, whereby those with the most significant ability to fulfil a desired function execute that function. For example, if we are unfortunate enough to undergo brain surgery, we presume that the surgeon has been selected because of her ability; her proven history of successful surgery. To the extent that we value our health and possibly life, her sexual, racial or gender diversity is of no consequence whatsoever. However, intersectionality shifts this guiding social logic and replaces ability with one of identity diversity, all to correct for an alleged historical deficit of some kind. To justify this shift in focus and the obvious ways it could lead to bad outcomes, a claim is made that diversity ensures optimal results. Across the corporate world in the Anglophone West, this claim is made time and again.[17]

This is spurious in several ways. A diverse workforce may produce optimal outcomes, but only if those within the workforce have been selected for ability. To the extent that the need for diversity has guided who is chosen to perform a job, suboptimal outcomes will inevitably be produced. Beyond this, any glance at some of the most successful human societies (measured in terms of wealth, quality of life etc.) are often very non-diverse: Japan being one example of many. Moreover, the most important element of diversity is opinion: many viewpoints may allow different perspectives on a problem to be assessed. However, how we proceed is directed by the integrity of the collective sum of knowledge. To extend our example, there may be numerous opinions on how to conduct brain surgery. Still, many will be wrong, and we need rationally to adjudicate the wrong from the right way of executing complex procedures and thus select the team to do the job.

Importantly, this claim for diversity is deeply problematic insofar as it posits an innate relationship between the identity of somebody and their worldview: what I called the correspondence theory of knowledge in the previous chapters. Why would somebody's ethnicity become the critical determining factor in their understanding? Is there such a thing as a 'black opinion' or sets of thoughts or ideas that only specific races can access? In short, to the extent that the quest for diversity takes primacy over merit, and when aggregated at the population level across society, we will see sub-optimal results time and time again.

Moreover, the claim that diversity is a strength is a statement of political faith, not fact.[18] Despite the attempts essentially to rewrite British history as a 'nation of immigrants' this is in fact a recent innovation, with the costs of absorption often borne by the poorest and most socially vulnerable communities. Diversity is just as likely to be accompanied by a reduction in social solidarity and multi-ethnic societies are often characterised by instability. The claim's veracity must be tested against specific metrics of strength or success, not merely asserted as a progressive catechism.

Second, beyond subverting the guiding apex values from ability to diversity, intersectionality also theoretically avoids privileging a specific vector of disadvantage as more determinative of one's life chances than another. However, in reality, race, gender and sexuality are ideologically privileged vectors within the ideology, with white, heterosexual men (incorrectly) placed at the top of the privilege pyramid and thus fair game for those enforcing intersectional ideology within organisations. Indeed, there is now a developing trend of managing what is said to be a 'zero-sum game mentality' among white men who feel they are being disadvantaged.[19] Similarly, in the university context, we can see that socio-economic class is largely ignored or considered a much lower priority.

This has had tremendous real-world effects, where institutions 'virtue signal' and seek external accreditation around issues considered to be of sacred importance to intersectional ideology but ignore the principal vectors of disadvantage, as they carry little ideological or reputational weight – for example, social class. As such, actual and growing disparities continue to grow and fester, while building wider social resentment, not least when coupled with the toxic mix of elite disdain, moral hectoring and real-world immiseration, with majority populations increasingly under-represented or actively managed out of institutions that have historically driven social mobility for all.

Given real-world data, there is a clear danger of increased resentment as disparities grow and institutions' garbled responses to political fads widen this divide. For example, and to give just one example of many, the elite Bristol University launched a one-million-pound scholarship programme to support 130 black students from 2021 onwards, totalling just under eight thousand pounds for each.[20] Conversely, to allow young people from traditionally deprived working-class backgrounds to access Bristol in its widening participation scheme, it instead offers scholarships of two thousand pounds each and, even then, one of Bristol's two widening participation schemes is exclusively for black applicants to their masters programmes.[21] Helping disadvantaged young people from any background is a great thing to do but, as the data clearly show, doing so on a racially selective basis, and in the context of the over-representation of BAME students, simply adds to further alienation and inequality and real-world disparities, given what the data clearly show and that university leaders cannot possibly not know. In short, despite the evidence of real-world disparity, virtue signalling and placating activists takes precedence over social mobility.

In the purview of modern identity politics, it is thus more than feasible that a female ethnic minority professor at Cambridge may be considered more oppressed than, for example, a white working-class university porter, given the various oppressive intersections of her racial or gender identity.[22] Indeed, according to woke intersectionalism, this does not matter: in a hypothetical example, a lecture hall composed of the diverse children of non-white billionaires is a more indicative form of social justice than one full of white young people drawn from the poorest state schools and the UK's council estates. For example, Azadeh Moshiri is now a senior journalist for BBC World News. Without the John Schofield Trust, a charity whose goal is to promote social mobility and greater diversity, she stated her career would never have happened. Her father is Farhad Moshiri, owner of Everton FC and worth an estimated £2.4 billion, while her mother is Nazenin Ansari, a journalist who has worked for the BBC, Sky News and CNN.

This accords with what the African American social theorist Shelby Steele argues is driving these deeper changes across American institutions and the Anglophone world more broadly: white guilt, which, he says, is a form of inverse racism. Holding ethnic minorities to the same standards as the white majority in this age of white guilt is 'synonymous with oppression'. As such, institutions 'live by a simple formula: lessening responsibility for minorities equals more authority; increasing it equals racism'. This reinforces a dangerous but sadly prevalent fallacy. 'Wherever and whenever there is white guilt, a terrible illusion prevails that social justice is not a condition but an agent.' This illusion reinforces the belief that social justice 'procures an entirely better life for people apart from their efforts', that in turn means minorities 'make social justice a priority over their individual pursuit of education and wealth'.[23]

We saw this logic in previous chapters, where universities have endorsed the theories of activists that seek to lessen people's responsibility in favour of racially coded special dispensation based on a fallacious racial conspiracy theory about the ubiquity of white privilege and structural racism. Steele captures it well. Suppose 'Marvin Gaye or Duke Ellington' or 'millions of other' ethnic minorities had let their 'pursuit of excellence be somehow contingent on the . . . spiritually withering interventions of needy, morally selfish white people betting on the cliché of black inferiority rather than on the natural human longing for excellence that resides in us all?'[24]

Racial, gender or sexual diversity is thus a form of performative social justice. It infantilises alleged victims and foregrounds a problematic theory of legacy oppressions to erase a focus on actual life chances and the transformative power of human agency and personal responsibility in addressing and overcoming obstacles to success.

In relation to the politics of race, progressives have sought to perpetuate a politics of grievance. This helps to corral ethnic minorities onto new moral 'plantations' predicated on perpetual victimhood, and who can then be utilised for the purposes of winning elections. For example, to maintain their share of the ethnic minority vote in California, and despite the fact the state did not support slavery, the Democrat's Gavin Newsom is currently seeking to pass a 'reparations' law to hand every black resident up to $200,000. The major debate now is whether the money should only go to the relatively tiny number of residents who can trace a lineage back to slavery, or whether all black people in California should receive the money. Helping to justify this more expansive hand-out based on race, arguments have included the fact that black homeowners' houses are said often to be worth less than those in majority white neighbourhoods.[25] In his scathing critique, Woodson terms this a form of 'race hustling'.[26]

## Woke capitalism

Wesley Yang terms the emergence of intersectionality a new successor ideology to the previous radical, primarily Marxist ideologies that historically dominated campus debates. He argues that this new woke successor ideology describes the 'melange of academic radicalism now seeking hegemony throughout American institutions' that has come to replace the post-war liberal consensus.[27] He further claims that the successor ideology focuses upon identitarianism but poses little threat of significant social or political change. In this, it is profoundly anti-radical, while posing as oppositional. This is perhaps one of the reasons why multinational corporations have widely adopted it; what has been termed 'woke capital'.[28] The term essentially refers to the phenomena whereby mainly American multinational corporations are increasingly incorporating social and political activism, particularly related to issues of race and social justice, into their marketing and branding strategies. This can take the form of corporate social responsibility initiatives, advertising campaigns that highlight the company's commitment to diversity and inclusion, and public statements in support of social-justice causes. Given their commanding heights at the top of the capitalist economy, why would these corporate behemoths champion ideas ostensibly associated with the progressive Left, who have historically been antithetical to corporate America? Several factors can explain this.

First, corporate virtue signalling around social-justice issues is a form of reputational Danegeld, itself a tax originally imposed in ancient England to pay off Viking raiders in the eleventh century. By signalling one's commitment publicly, woke capital can thus make the right noises to display their ethical obligations to social-media activists and increasingly social-justice focused shareholders. For example, some of the US's largest multinational corporations have come under increased criticism for their political activism and performative commitment to social-justice issues.[29] Performative, as in practice, like many multinationals, a number are alleged to have used widespread slave labour in the Xinjiang province in China.[30]

In the UK context, to maintain the lucrative international student market during the Covid pandemic, UK universities changed their teaching materials to deliver online teaching content, most notably to China. There was a slight catch in that online students from China could only access reading material on a list allowed by the censors of China's Communist Party. Thus, universities decolonised the curriculum for the sins of yesterday's aristocrats, while recolonising the curriculum for the sons and daughters of today's CCP and Chinese elite.[31] In the case of Cambridge, one of the UK's leading universities, the close relationship between the university authorities and China's political elites has reached worrying proportions.[32] Perhaps an actual test of virtue and commitment to social justice would be to act or speak out when the costs to one's interests are high?

As Yang concludes, intersectional woke ideology has been 'easily adopted by those at the commanding heights of our capitalist system'. It is a way of signalling virtue, while resisting any form of more profound political changes. The key indicator of social justice, Yang argues, is thus a form of 'proportional representation within the ownership class, within the upper reaches of the managerial classes of various identities' and not meaningful social or political changes.[33]

Similarly, Kaufman develops a value taxonomy between what he calls 'cultural liberalism' and 'cultural socialism'. Cultural liberalism is based on post-war norms around freedom, pluralism and equality before the law. He argues that it emphasises freedom of expression and that individuals 'should not be compelled to endorse beliefs that they oppose and should be treated equally by social norms and the law'. In contrast, he terms cultural socialism 'the idea that public policy should be used to redistribute wealth, power, and self-esteem from the privileged groups in society to disadvantaged groups, especially racial and sexual minorities and women. This justifies restrictions on the freedom and equal treatment of members of advantaged groups.'[34]

For Kaufman, cultural socialism closely resembles a form of religion, with its sacred beliefs and original sins, such as whiteness, and redemption and salvation through the recognition of whiteness and recanting of one's white privilege, to be born again as an 'ally' and through 'allyship' with minority groups that are sacralised. In a pun on the historical Great Awakenings of American Christianity, Matthew Yglesias referred to this phenomenon as the 'Great Awokening'.[35] As such, wokeness is emerging as the established faith in the legal and regulatory framework of the American political system, as well as in elite corporate culture and academia in the broader Anglophone West. This secular religiosity of wokeness helps partially explain the intensity of its advocates, a theme picked up by the leading African American linguist, John McWhorter. In the case of the US, he argues that contemporary 'anti-racism' is a new religion, led by what he calls the 'elect', a theme echoed by Doyle, who see the proselytisers of this form of social-justice activism as the new puritans.[36]

In its emphasis on identity, Yang argues that wokery is thus a form of 'authoritarian Utopianism that masquerades as liberal humanism while usurping it from within'.[37] Wokery presents itself as a progressive and liberal ideology that is focused on promoting equality and justice, but it is an authoritarian and utopian ideology that seeks to impose its own vision of society on others. He also suggests that wokery is attempting to 'usurp' or take over liberal humanism from within, implying that it is seeking to replace traditional liberal values with its own ideology. This is an important point. As we have seen in previous chapters, modern wokery as manifest in the Anglophone world's culture wars has become actively hostile to core Enlightenment and liberal values, including pluralism, freedom of speech, colour blindness, equality of opportunity and the importance of the individual.[38] Reversing the philosophy of

Martin Luther King, it is not interested in the content of one's character but instead on one's group identity. The underlying goal is to achieve a form of social justice measured by the technocratic imposition of equal outcomes (equity) for victim groups sacralised and placed within an ideological intersectional matrix of structural oppression. This has now assumed a central place in the Biden administration's policy programme, and across Western institutions more generally.

The rejection and active opposition to liberal norms is explicit and made clear by some of its chief theorists. As the bestselling CRT theorists Robin DiAngelo and Özlem Sensoy argue, the 'logic of individual autonomy that underlies liberal humanism (the idea that people are free to make independent rational decisions that determine their own fate)' is a 'mechanism for keeping the marginalised in their place by obscuring larger structural systems of inequality. In other words, it fooled people into believing that they had more freedom and choice than societal structures actually allow.'[39] As part of this ideology and to explain the more general hostility to white majorities in both the US and the UK, white majorities are said to have a material interest in racism and their own 'whiteness', which it is claimed, delivers them privileges. As outlined by CRT's leading theorists, all white people have what they term an 'interest convergence' as 'racism advances the interests of both white elites (materially) and working-class people (psychically)' and thus have 'little incentive to eradicate it'.[40] It is perhaps astonishing that an ideology so vehemently opposed to liberal norms can be so enthusiastically adopted across the Anglophone West.

Perhaps this view of the white working class as unreconstructed racists also helps explain their continued under-participation in UK universities and the lack of commitment to equality on the part of university technocrats? In the next section, I examine how and why this has become the case.

## Globalisation and the managerial class

As the political economy of the Anglophone West changed in the 1970s, a new managerial class emerged. In an early analysis of these new elites, Barbara and John Ehrenreich termed this new elite a Professional-Managerial Class (PMC) who took advantage of the unwinding of the post-war settlement that had broadly benefited the working class.[41] This settlement included a welfare state, nationalisation, and strong trade unions all anchored around a cohesive nation state committed to a bounded political community. This consensus was broken in the Anglophone economies from the late 1970s onwards and reached its apogee in the era of globalisation. In this new era, jobs were offshored, mainly to East Asia, and economies increasingly moved from manufacturing (and the settled communities that sprang up around heavy industry) to a service economy and mass immigration to help create 'labour flexibility', both of which often changed the demographic make-up and the cultural norms of extended settled communities. In short, social cohesion and nation states were increasingly superseded by new forms of 'globalism' and the emergence of a new elites to manage these transitions.

More importantly, a new hierarchical cultural and moral order emerged under this form of hyper-liberal globalism managed by these new PMCs. Instead of what some might see as outdated ideas of nationhood and social cohesion, the new moral hierarchy instead emphasised individualism and self-discovery over that of the community and self-sacrifice. It rewarded those whose personal identity centred around ethical flexibility. It also benefited those whose education enabled geographic mobility to take advantage of this increasingly borderless world, mainly credentialed elites and those who could quickly shift to mitigate the negative externalities (real or imagined) of the effects of these sweeping changes.

In a scathing critique, Catherine Liu argued this PMC thus has its social power, status and growing economic leverage invested in a very different moral order to that of the more traditional and soon-to-be-left-behind communities that either could not or would not be able to access the kinds of cultural institutions that acted as a conveyor belt for the PMC. In the UK context, Goodhart characterises this as a new divide between the 'anywheres', who have 'achieved' identities, derived from their careers and education, and the 'somewheres', who get their identity from a sense of place and the people around them, and who feel a sense of loss due to the fragmentation imposed by globalisation and rapid social change. These new PMC elites champion progressive causes and seek morally to police working-class political agency.[42]

Accompanying this new moral and cultural order, overseen by the new PMC, was a form of democratic capture through increased supranationalism, where decision making (accompanying the offshoring of manufacturing and the liquidity of capital) was upscaled to structures of governance that escaped the nation state and thus democratic national decision making. The social power of this PMC was thus secured within supranational forms of technocratic administration, and suitably protected from national democratic accountability. Instead, decisions were transmitted down to the nation state, and then dissipated across 'one step removed' forms of quasi-autonomous governance within the nation state itself. Democracy was thus hollowed out, and upscaled to forms of international governance that was insulated from popular mandate. Domestic political representatives thus outsourced their political responsibilities with domestic politics more akin to a form of performative political theatre captured today by the centrality of social media in driving the political agenda.

This form of democratic neutering has been justified as the lumpen masses are cast as inexplicably resistant to progressive dogma. The promotion of the political hegemony of contemporary progressivism is thus removed from the domain of politics and democratic consent and, instead, presented legalistically as 'human rights', justified under the rubric of an endless struggle to protect vulnerable groups. The PMC does not see politics as the struggle to win democratic consent for its ideas but, instead, the suppression of popular will justified as necessary to allow the natural and inevitable progressive arc of history to unfold. Left-wing politics used to be based on upholding the rights, interests and instincts of the common man and woman; now seen as little more than explosions of 'vulgar populism', which must be corralled, contained and neutered.

In a scathing analysis, Deneen argues that 'identities and diversity thus secured are globally homogenous, the precondition for a fungible global elite, who readily identify other members capable of living in a cultureless and placeless world, defined above all by liberal norms of globalised indifference toward shared fates of actual neighbors and communities'. He continues that one of the 'most powerful ways that liberalism advances is by implicitly encouraging globalised narcissism, while perpetuating a pervasive belief in its benevolence. Those who remain in the hamlets, towns and cities are generally condemned to straitened economic circumstances, destined for low-wage and stagnant service industry jobs and cut off from the top tier of analytic-conceptual work that is reserved for elite graduates.'[43]

Middle Americans as they appear to the PMC; the 'makers of educated opinion', argues Lasch, are 'hopelessly shabby, unfashionable, and provincial, ill-informed about changes in taste or intellectual trends . . . They are at once absurd and vaguely menacing – not because they wish to overthrow the old order but precisely because of their defense of it.'[44] Lind extends this and argues that education is the crucial fault line in a class-based culture war between an educated and often over-credentialed PMC overclass and left-behind underclass.[45]

As such, populism as manifest in forms of working-class protest against the cultural and political hegemony of globalisation and the PMC is nothing new. Indeed, it is an 'ongoing counterrevolution from below against the half-century-long technocratic neoliberal revolution from above imposed by Western managerial elites'.

In this, this elite came to see itself as opposed to everything the more bounded communities embodied, including their stubborn refusal to abandon perceived gauche notions of nationhood, patriotism and borders: 'deplorables' to use Hilary Clinton's now infamous line or 'semi-fascists' to use Biden's current terminology. In the UK, Brexit was primarily a working-class revolt against the new globalised political economy and its attendant worldview of open borders and supranationalism generated similar comparisons. For example, pro-Brexit working-class voters were castigated as white 'gammons', flushed red in their incandescent and right-wing media-duped rage over immigration, as a political adviser to former Labour leader Jeremy Corbyn explained.[46]

Recent polling data suggest that this class disdain is growing. For example, US polling shows that educated and progressive white liberals, the key adherents of intersectional successor ideology, are becoming ever more hostile to the white working class.[47] Ironically, white progressives are much more enthusiastic about the idea that diversity makes the United States a better place to live than blacks or Latinos. 'In the past five years, white liberals have moved so far to the left on questions of race and racism that they are now, on these issues, to the left of even the typical "black voter"', Yglesias asserts.[48] Interestingly, these trends preceded the divisive Presidency of Donald Trump.

## Munchausen syndrome by progressive proxy

How can we relate the above more generally to the new politics of 'anti-racism' that we have examined in this book and its assault on British universities and institutions? First, I believe that the moral panic over racism in British institutions reflects the fact that the power of the PMC is primarily advanced through a form of governance centred around moral policing and forms of therapeutic authoritarianism.

Specifically, the new 'anti-racism' that emerged in the post-Floyd era grows out of a general shift in progressive politics in the UK, whereby moralising coalitions and alliances are created by emphasising identity and real or manufactured forms of grievance politics. As Lasch argues, these new moral coalitions help sustain the power of technocratic professional managerial elites. As globalisation has transformed the Anglophone political economies along the lines we saw above, the old politics of Left and Right has given way to a new moral economy that has replaced pivotal questions of economic redistribution.[49] 'On both sides of the Atlantic, national elites have promoted the technocratic neoliberal vision of a glorious globalised future of dissolving borders, free migration of goods and people and ever-growing demographic diversity – combined, it was assumed, with monolithically liberal values and opinions.'[50]

The visible signalling around an institution's 'uplift' or championing of the interests of historically oppressed groups has a number of uses. By assuming responsibility and thus the political power for 'fixing' issues of alleged burning injustice, PMC cadres in UK universities reassert the moral authority of the institutions they run, and that have lost their practical authority. It is useful to see this as a form of Munchausen syndrome by progressive proxy that is a type of abuse in which a caregiver, usually a parent, fabricates, exaggerates, or induces physical or psychological symptoms in a person under their care, such as a child, an elderly adult, or a person with a disability. The caregiver then seeks medical treatment for the fabricated or induced symptoms. Second, this form of 'caregiving' also cements their power through ethical signalling. The moral panics that have gripped and restructured UK universities should be seen in this context: a form of ethical entrepreneurialism to sustain bureaucratic power and breathe life and moral directionality into what are little more than multi-billion-pound education businesses, operating in a cut-throat marketplace.

Second, this grievance politics also conveniently elides with the kinds of post-national cultural order examined above. Alternative placeless solidarity is assumed, along with a hierarchy that divides the educated (enlightened) post-national citizen from the lumpen and uneducated (unenlightened) citizen within nations. Social phenomena and normative legitimacy are thus defined by the world experiences of (usually white) upper middle-class professionals, with everyone else castigated as biased, or in need of education, should they dare to question this ideological hegemony. In the context of the 2020 election, then Democratic presidential nominee Joe Biden even went so far as to state that if 'you have a problem figuring out whether you're for me or Trump, then you ain't black'.[51]

This moral economy is ideally suited to supranationalism, placelessness and the rejection of bounded communities, rooted in generational solidarity. Contemporary progressive anti-racism, alongside other grievance politics, is the moral condition of possibility for national deconstruction, where the nation is seen as a depository of all that is backward and wrong. In short, 'if the nation is fundamentally racist, sexist and homophobic, I owe it nothing. More than that, conscience demands that I repudiate it.'[52]

In a scathing piece on how the politics of anti-racism allows an easy way to signal virtue, while being insulated from the effects of one's proposed solutions, Crawford argues that virtue no longer consists of what you 'do or don't do; it consists of having the correct opinions. This is attractive, as one may then exempt oneself from the high-minded policies one inflicts upon everyone else.' In the American context, 'schools are turned into laboratories of grievance-based social engineering, with generally disastrous effects, but you send your own children to expensive private schools. You can de-legitimise the police out of a professed concern for black people, and the explosion of murder will be confined to black parts of the city you never see and in which journalists are not interested. In this way, you can be magnanimous, while avoiding the moral pollution that comes from noticing reality.'[53]

In the UK context, we can see how politics played out in the Brexit debates. Less a rational cost-versus-benefit analysis, and more akin to a theological battle, it showed with clarity that when ordinary people exercise their political agency in ways that are antithetical to the moral economy of technocratic progressivism, they are portrayed as brainwashed dupes.

The populist reaction against these technocratic elites partially explains the rise of Trumpism in the US and, though it differs in meaningful ways, the politics of Brexit in the UK. In short, the culture war is waged by technocratic elites against ordinary people. It is, in fact and outcome, a form of status class war, designed to maintain power through manipulating a politics of grievance and bureaucratic mission, advanced through proclamations of social vulnerability from which populations need to be protected (microaggressions, the wrong thoughts and so on).

Identifying and protecting alleged vulnerable groups is essential, as it allows the PMC to promote relentless anxiety across social life. Vulnerable groups are used to create a sense of constant anxiety in society. This fear of potential risks allows for the justification of increased regulation and control in all areas of life. The prevention of these perceived risks gives power to those in positions of authority and allows them to justify their rule. This perma-crisis of catastrophisation thus normalises the invocation of vulnerability, and the prevention of the materialisation of these risks gives moral clout and political justification for PMC rule. As Ramsay argues, politics is thus reconstituted as a conflict between competing claims of vulnerability, with much of progressive politics now little more than a call for various forms of public or private authority to police the speech, opinions and behaviour of alleged oppressor groups to protect the marginalised identities of what are cast as endlessly vulnerable populations.[54]

In this, suffering becomes a commodity, often monetised and thus suffused with vested interests. As Furedi argues, allegations of vulnerability and emotional harm have become the central cultural resources through which students, and increasingly members of the academic community, express their identity or make statements about their plight.[55] As such, distress or intellectual challenge are coded as forms of emotional injury, with the language of trauma and psychological harm invoked concerning seemingly banal interactions or events such as taking some stairs, using the wrong body language, or not maintaining eye contact while in conversation. These demons, thus conjured, require exorcism by technocratic inquisitors, well-renumerated EDI consultancies and politically motivated activists who invoke trauma and emotional damage to help drive the agenda. Through this lens, we can understand the growing illiberalism inherent in campus cultures in the UK and the politics of weaponised moral panics. In short, it is a power play wrapped in a trauma shield: obey me and do as I tell you, or you will harm vulnerable groups and I will seek to cast you out.

I have argued throughout this book that what happens on UK campuses is very important. Universities shape the minds of future elites. What happens on the campus today will thus directly impact the UK tomorrow. This is also not just about culture in the domestic sense. As I have shown, decolonial activists and woke ideologists seek a seeming total repudiation of Western civilisation. It is not clear what kind of end state they desire but, given the close relationship between a nation's sense of identity and history and the seeming pervasiveness of intersectionalism across British institutional life, this has profound ramifications beyond Britain's shores. The UK has long been a central 'custodian' state of the liberal international order. How a nation understands itself impacts the moral purpose and confidence it can bring to bear on projecting those values internationally. In the final chapter of this book, I draw out these more profound issues of identity, foreign policy and geopolitics.

# Conclusion:
# The future of the West?

By their very nature, historical narratives are often highly potent in shaping national self-understanding. They thus carry profound political significance. Within our centres of learning, arguably the most important cultural institutions, given their capacity to shape young minds, I have shown how wokery and the politics of Western repudiation are prevalent. New forms of bureaucratic authoritarianism are being instituted, young minds are coddled, and a divisive ideology undermines equality, pluralism and freedom.

The implications of this are significant, as these developments are intimately bound up with the future of the Western-led 'liberal international order' itself. This is because a state's foreign and domestic policy draws from a more profound cultural story that is inextricably linked to national identity: before any nation can act, it needs to know what it is. These cultural stories enable and constrain action as powerfully as (if not more than) military or financial capabilities. They describe our place in the world, help order social relationships between citizens and the state, and give purpose and meaning to action.

In short, a cultural story of who we are is necessary for politics, the purposeful structuring of human agency to attain what we want. A nation is not just a place but a collective story that binds, unifies and links the past with the present, to map a future. This is one of the key reasons the culture wars are so important. These are struggles over meaning, identity and social purpose. We are living through a time when our traditional institutions seem to be on the road to the active denigration of British history and the repudiation of the merits, indeed the very right to exist, of Western civilisation itself. This form of self-denigration and repudiation is dangerous.

The UK has been integral to maintaining the liberal international order in the post-war period. This order emerged from the ashes of the Second World War and European colonial dissolution. It recognised that in its natural state, international relations are little more than a 'jungle' with no umpire to ensure fair play or global police force to punish wrongdoers. Prevaricate or show weakness, and you risk being picked off and consumed by bigger beasts; this is the relentless historical dynamic of world politics and is illustrated most recently by Russia's brutal war in Ukraine.

For most of human history, the strong have done as they will, while the weak suffer what they must. We have examined many examples of this in this book. States have dominated other states that were too weak to resist encroachment. In many ways, the post-war liberal international order, underpinned by American military power and supported by the UK, especially in the European continent, was an attempt to mitigate this remorseless logic. It was never perfect, and there were many shades of grey, with the US often hypocritically violating its liberal norms, especially in the global South in the Cold War context.

Still, it recognised that the form of international order that prevails is intimately related to the domestic norms of those states upholding that order. Domestic norms, a people's sense of history and how this informs national identity and purpose, matter greatly. Think, for example, of the kind of international order we would live under if Hitler had won the Second World War.

During this conflict, as states vied for hegemony, tens of millions were killed, and human suffering was on scales almost beyond imagination. After the war ended, Great Britain, the world's previous hegemon, was effectively bankrupt, and the baton for world leadership passed inexorably from the Pax Britannica to a Pax Americana. This transition was underpinned by the concentration of power in America's hands. From the ruins of the Second World War, America's industrial capacity remained untouched; it possessed vast reserves of capital, it had a military power unmatched in human history and it enjoyed regional hegemony across the Americas.

Unusual in history, however, and unlike previous great powers that have emerged victorious after significant conflicts, America did not use this new-found power to construct a form of global colonial order that sought the decimation of the losers, formal territorial occupation or other forms of 'bounty' that victors often claim. The architects of the post-war order sought to use America's new-found superpower status to construct a world order that reflected the domestic values of America itself: a liberal international order, in the first instance, geographically bound to western Europe and a Japan-centred East Asia.

At the heart of this US-led liberal post-war architecture was a quid pro quo. In return for recognising that the US was now the undisputed king of the jungle, both former enemies and its now subordinate allies would play by its rules. And, while economic competition would take place (with Japan and Germany challenging US economic hegemony as early as the 1970s), none would challenge the US militarily or embark on military adventures without permission (as the British learnt to their peril during the Suez crisis of 1956).[1] In return, states within the US-led liberal order would have access to US markets and capital, as well as sets of US-led institutions to regularise political-economic interactions and a rules-based system that would give voice to weaker states and forms of complex interdependence to international relations.[2]

This deal also contained a security component. If you were in the 'liberal club', you would also enjoy US security protection. For Japan, this was codified within the US–Japan Security Pact and the North Atlantic Treaty Organization (NATO) for the Europeans.[3] The US security guarantee not only checked and contained the threat of Soviet tyranny but also alleviated geopolitics in these critical regions. Japan would grow economically but no longer threaten its neighbours militarily, which helped with regional economic integration. In Europe, US military power became the security precondition for the complex forms of political and economic interdependence built up in the post-war period, with the US as the key architect of European integration. Lord Hastings, NATO's first Secretary General, famously declared that the alliance was designed to 'keep the Soviet Union out, the Americans in, and the Germans down'. Alongside these benefits, the security provided by the US also allowed the Europeans to build up large welfare states, not least because they did not have to foot the bill for their protection. Europe's historical balance of power between its great powers of France, Germany and the UK was also resolved through the subordination of their security to America's superintendence and forms of security 'free riding'.

After the end of the Cold War, NATO and the EU expanded into the former Soviet sphere of influence, and rising East Asian powers joined global institutions such as the World Trade Organization. The liberal order became the institutional instantiation of the US's global ambitions: world trade, a peaceful (and subordinated) Europe, and states in East Asia that looked to the US for security. Of course, they also had to accept that as hegemon, the US occasionally acted unilaterally to defend its national interests, as we saw in the imbroglios in Iraq and Afghanistan.

Today, we have complex forms of global economic inter-dependence, sets of global institutions and an international system that is more ordered and pacific. This may sound strange as Russia's war in Ukraine continues and China eyes Taiwan, but the balance of power remains on the side of the democratic West; however, that is now changing.

Reflecting Hobbes's refrain that covenants without the sword are but words and of no strength to secure a man, the ironic reality is that the progressive faith in a flat borderless world always rested on this highly contingent post-1945 settlement, underpinned by Western hegemony. Indeed, most of the theorists invoked by decolonisation activists lived and worked in elite institutions in the West. As such, forms of pacific and interconnected international orders have been the anomaly and not the norm in human history. Rather than the EU, the post-war European peace of the last seventy years has been sustained by US and UK security guarantees in NATO and the resolution of German continental hegemony through constitutionalising its power within a pan-European superstructure.

Through this lens, the impulse of the UK's Brexit can be interpreted as a return to the importance of national sovereignty in an increasingly post-liberal world order, where geopolitics and great power competition are making a rapid comeback. Following the Covid-19 pandemic and China's growing military power, the global economy will likely revert to a bipolar world that, from a trade perspective, will appear something like the Cold War stand-off between the Soviet Union's Council for Mutual Economic Assistance trading bloc and the US-led Organisation for Economic Cooperation and Development (OECD) trading area, with developing countries siding with one or the other as they see fit.

What would this mean for the UK? If the world divides into competing regional trading blocs – arguably the more likely outcome – Britain would doubtless join the US bloc for economic and national security reasons. So, too, would the EU, Japan, Australia and New Zealand. Competition for secure sources of supplies would be fierce. Life would not be comfortable. World politics is now exiting the era of unipolar globalisation under the superintendence of American power.

The situation within the US trading bloc might resemble the nineteenth-century world, where states competed through forming their 'national champion' companies to access supplies. In the twenty-first century, competition would be through overseas direct investment rather than formal colonisation. In a post-pandemic world, with likely deep fissures within the liberal economic order: the 'national interest' will come to be the policy makers' guiding light, rather than a moral compass.

If we accept that one of the prerequisites for the rise of challengers to the West, such as Russia and China, is a degree of confidence and civilisational 'mojo', where does that leave the UK? What does the West now offer to counter these highly illiberal and often authoritarian states and social forces? What social glue holds free and open countries together with a common purpose to defend their shared institutional order, upon which their rights and freedoms – all highly fragile and historically contingent – now rest?

From the People's Republic of China's (PRC) growing global ambition, Russia's desire for systemic revision or the continuing threat from radical Islamist insurgencies, the 'open international order' – in the British Integrated Review – is assailed on many external fronts.[4] While these anti-Western states and social forces differ, their global purpose shares a common historical thread. These include a sense of loss due to the malign agency of the West, the need to overturn the Anglo-American-led order and a belief that, in so doing, a return to greater status will follow. Within this anti-Western narrative, an historical discourse on the role of the British Empire assumes a symbolic place. For example, the depiction

of China's loss of Hong Kong to the British as part of a long history of its 'humiliation and the people's sorrow', according to
Xi Jinping, General Secretary of the Chinese Communist Party
(CCP), has been used to justify the PRC's present crackdown in
the former British territory.[5]

As Biggar argues, this is strategic: 'If you want to make others
obey your will, it is useful to subvert their self-confidence and
weaponise guilt.' Guilt is one of the most powerful and disa-
bling human emotions. He continues that if 'Henry Kissinger
is to be believed, since Sun Tzu's *Art of War* in the fifth century
BCE, Chinese *realpolitik* has placed a premium on gaining
psychological advantage. Certainly, illiberal states are looking
to gain that now. In 2011 a British diplomat in China was told:
'What you have to remember is that you come from a weak and
declining nation.' And when, in July 2020, Britain criticised the
Chinese regime for running roughshod over the Sino-British
Joint Declaration of 1984, in which the PRC had agreed to
respect Hong Kong's relative autonomy and liberal rights until
2047, Beijing's ambassador was quick to dismiss the criticism
as 'colonial interference'.[6]

This is underlined by the fact that China has sought to
weaponise wokery to attack the West and undercut its 'soft
power' and sense of moral purpose. For example, China's
'United Front Work Department' has over 40,000 active
personnel. It engages in public diplomacy and propaganda
as part of its efforts to promote the interests of the Chinese
Communist Party (CCP) both domestically and abroad. This
includes efforts to shape foreign perceptions of China and
the CCP, as well as to influence foreign governments, media
organisations and other influential groups. It also works to
build relationships with foreign individuals and organisations
that are supportive of China's interests and to encourage them
to speak out in favour of China. Purportedly, one of its key
strategies is exacerbating racial tension and weakening media
integrity in the West.[7]

Chinese Premier Xi Jinping argued that the Work Front remained an 'important magic weapon for realising the China Dream of the Great Rejuvenation of the Chinese Nation'.[8] In his first high-level delegation with China, President Biden was admonished by Yang Jiechi, director of the Central Foreign Affairs Commission of the Chinese Communist Party. Yang argued that Biden should not criticise China's stance on human rights as the 'fact is that there are many problems within the United States regarding human rights, which is admitted by the United States itself as well . . . the challenges facing the United States in human rights are deep-seated. They did not just emerge over the past four years, such as Black Lives Matter.'[9] In its editorial, China's *Global Times* followed up with a statement that 'Washington has always twisted the facts. It has been bragging about its allies. As it undermines the rules, it is also blatantly promoting a so-called rules-based international order. Everything Washington talks about is centred on the US, and on white supremacy. The interests of the US and its few allies have become the starting point of right and wrong.'[10]

Castigating the Anglosphere intelligence sharing arrangement called 'Five Eyes' between the US, Canada, the UK and Australia, Chinese media argued that this is, in fact, a 'US-centred, racist, and mafia-styled community, wilfully and arrogantly provoking China and trying to consolidate their hegemony as all gangsters do. They are becoming a racist axis aimed at stifling the development rights of 1.4 billion Chinese.' It goes on to note that members of the Five Eyes alliance 'are all English-speaking countries. The formation of four states, except the UK, is the result of British colonisation. Those countries share the Anglo-Saxon civilisation [now] targeting China and Russia. The evil idea of racism has been fermenting consciously or unconsciously in their clashes with the two countries.'[11]

Putin's Russia has also weaponised wokery. In past presidential campaigns for example, Russian operatives 'used

inaccurate and misleading information in a coordinated campaign to manipulate public opinion and disrupt the political
process ... Many of these posts addressed race and social-
justice issues. To maximise the divisiveness of these posts,
Russian operatives often shared competing positions on these
issues.'[12] A St Petersburg-based 'troll farm' deployed social
media accounts, some labelled 'Woke Blacks' and 'Blacktivists'.
Oxford University's Computational Propaganda Project concluded that Russian political messaging to 'African Americans
sought to divert their political energy away from established
political institutions by preying on anger with structural inequalities.'[13] Russian Foreign Minister Lavrov stated that Russia
categorically rejects 'the neocolonial "rules-based order" being
imposed by the US-led West. This order provides for a racist
division of the world into a privileged group of countries who
*a priori* have the right of any action and the rest of the world,
obliged to follow the tracks of this "golden billion" and service their interests.'[14] Instead, Russian foreign-policy makers
have attempted to portray Moscow's desire to revise the
Western-led rules-based order as a part of its championing of
global diversity against American imperialism. 'Our African
colleagues perfectly understand the root cause of what is hap-
pening, which is the collective West's attempt to slow down
the objective historical process, the formation of a just, democratic order, and cling to the elusive prospect of the so-called
unipolar world', Lavrov stated on an official visit to Ethiopia in
2022.[15]

Illiberal and authoritarian states are thus seeking to exploit
woke narratives to advance their own interests. This is not to
argue that all is perfect in the UK or the Anglophone West, but
this book has argued that the UK is a successful multi-racial
liberal democracy. Moreover, the still US-led liberal international order has been remarkable in its capacity to advance
human freedom, however stuttering that advance has been.
From the defeat of Hitler's racially genocidal regime and the

authoritarian Soviet Union, the open-market model it has helped promote has seen an incredible transformation of the global economy that has lifted billions from misery.

For example, in 1981, 44% of the world's population lived in extreme poverty. Since then, the world's share of impoverished people has declined faster than ever. In thirty-two years, the percentage of people living in extreme poverty had dropped to a staggering 10% by 2015. This is astonishing given the incredible growth of the world's population, from one billion in 1800 to eight billion today. This has been possible not least because of the remarkable economic developments in East Asia and the Pacific, where poverty rates went from 81% in 1981 to 2.3% in 2015.[16] In the less- and least-developed countries, child mortality has halved in the last twenty years.[17] The proliferation of online education platforms and telemedicine services has made it easier for people to access education and healthcare services, even in remote or underserved areas. Moreover, the development and widespread adoption of new communications technologies, such as the internet and mobile phones have helped to connect people around the world, facilitating the exchange of ideas and information and improving communication and access to information.

As I have argued, this shift in humanity's fortunes has been related to the values that wokery seeks to deconstruct: science, pluralism and free enquiry. This is a risky move in several ways. First, these values, as historically imperfectly applied as they may have been, have formed the basis for civil rights and human emancipation in the West. Frederick Douglass, born a slave and one of America's greatest orators and campaigners for freedom, captured it well. 'Liberty is meaningless where the right to utter one's thought and opinions has ceased to exist … Thrones, dominions, principalities, and powers, founded in injustice and wrong, are sure to tremble, if men are allowed to reason of righteousness, temperance, and of a judgment to come in their presence. Slavery cannot tolerate free speech.'[18]

From the abolitionist campaign to the civil rights movement in America, the noble cause of anti-racism has been advanced through solidarity across races. The fight against the injustice of racial discrimination was rooted in a vision of our common humanity and what bound us together.

Second, the relatively benign conditions enjoyed in the post-war Western world are not the historical norm. In an era structurally predisposed to a greater need for national cohesion and purpose in the face of coming challenges, the call for national abasement will undoubtedly face a political reckoning. As we see an increased bifurcation in the global economy and shifts in power away from the West to a dynamic East Asia, the Western political economy will suffer further severe dislocations. We will likely face the greater threat of interstate war as the world economy decouples. As we shift from an era of US unipolarity and global economic growth, hard questions that will likely often require hard answers will be engendered by the struggle over resources and a return of great power politics. To help carry us through, it is almost beyond comprehension that British institutions would continue to peddle a worldview based on the denigration of British history and thus civilisational purpose. The continued endorsement of a divisive form of collective racial guilt by what are privileged elites and relatively tiny minorities of self-interested activists is an indulgent dalliance in the context of Western decline.

Third, there are many dangers in the woke experiment. The Enlightenment idea was based in the belief that authority is grounded in humanity's shared rationality, with a common culture accessible in principle to every citizen and capable of articulation. However, technocratic progressivism requires the disqualification of experience and common sense as a guide to reality.[19] In that, we are now closer to the Enlightenment's caricature of a medieval society of a priestly form of authority based on the presumption of inner guilt, a telos of unallayed grievance and the primacy of emotion and lived experience over that which is real. Logic and reason are not tools of white supremacy, but instead a *via media* that allowed humans to escape the friend–enemy distinction common to politics; they are the foundations upon which we build together.

Fourth, we must not forget that human beings have a natural tendency towards tribalism. The steady cultivation of tolerance and mutual respect must be learnt and transmitted anew to each generation through our institutions and broader culture. By amping up the friend–enemy distinction, wokery erases the neutral space of civility that the Enlightenment tried to create.

New divisive thinking predicated around racial interest articulation is beginning to emerge from what is little more than anti-white racism peddled by 'critical race theorists' in our universities, media and boardrooms. Like children playing with fire while atop a tinder box, it reproduces a morality tale of minorities as vulnerable and defenseless and whose interests will be uplifted by benevolent and privileged progressives. As West notes, however, the 'villains of these tales were invariably the native poor, whose lack of enthusiasm for the newcomers, expressed without eloquence or sensitivity, was often a feature of media portrayals of integration'.[20] This seems to be the underlying gamble: elite guilt-tripping of a generalised majority population will lead to a cultural transformation in an historically inevitable progressive direction. However, the progressive perspective on history is not a factual account, but rather a theory or belief. It is a myth. Freedom is never free, but must be remade over and again, and then defended.

Moreover, this form of historical guilt tripping will likely not go far beyond the BBC, university lecture halls and other privileged islands. It is hard to see how the woke priesthood's catechism of white privilege and British self-flagellation will be received in left-behind post-industrial wastelands that char-acterise large parts of the UK. The moral evaluation of people in flagrantly inconsistent ways, depending on whether they are sociologically classified as oppressed according to intersectional ideology, places our current multi-racial dispensation in grave peril. This asymmetry not only grates against any sense of fairness. Multiculturalism cannot function if everybody is not treated the same.

Witness, for example, the jarring silence about the mass rape of vulnerable young and predominantly white girls on almost industrial levels by British-Pakistani men. The Independent Inquiry into Child Sexual Abuse in a report into these organised networks found that whether through a 'misplaced sense of political correctness or the sheer complexity of the problem', data collection that would have allowed more effective police intervention was inhibited, especially 'on ethnicity'.[21] These double standards are also clearly at play in terms of the targets of progressive moral outrage, in cases, for example, where Muslim faith leaders oppose homosexuality.[22] Think, for example, if the races of those committing mass rape were reversed. Is it conceivable to think that authorities would have not investigated sooner, or the terrible events would not be (rightly) subject to numerous reports, news coverage, documentaries and so on? In short, how long will ordinary people put up with being denigrated, told their country is beyond redemption and accept forms of elite restructuring of the institutions they hold dear in ways that are asymmetrically applied, deeply hypocritical and blatantly ideological?

Compounding this danger is what will likely be the future of mass migration to Europe and the UK. For example, Africa's population growth in the last fifty years has been unprecedented, and by the middle of the twenty-first century, the continent will make up a quarter of the global population. This population will be young. In Africa today, almost 60% of its population is younger than twenty-five years old, what Paice calls a 'youthquake'.[23] ONS figures from 2022 show annual net migration to the UK rose to an incredible 504,000 in the year to June 2022.[24]

As economic power shifts to the East, coupled with a steep rise in mass legal and illegal migration to the UK, the deal being offered seems to be that British citizens must now compete with the world's richest on the housing market and the world's poorest on the labour market within the context of crumbling services. Any criticism of these transformations is often labelled as racist and not allowed to be debated, or is justified as wholly positive by cheerleaders for these profound social transformations, often as a form of karmic payback for the injustices of the British Empire.

Relations are already strained. In the US, there is now a growing 'empathy gap' between people of different ethnicities, following the murder of George Floyd.[25] Forcing people to take unconscious bias tests increases racial biases.[26] Two years after George Floyd's murder, Americans' concerns about race relations remain elevated.[27] As UK elites have imported and championed America's toxic ideology of cultural intersectionality, there is already clear evidence that the UK's race relations have also worsened in the post-Floyd era. Nineteen per cent of the UK population thought that before the BLM protests, race relations were deteriorating. Since the protest and riots, that figure has risen to 36%.[28] Moreover, anti-immigration Left party voters are considerably more likely to switch to Right-leaning parties than pro-immigration Right party voters are to switch to a Left party like Labour.[29]

The West's long post-1945 boom, which helped fund the welfare state and universities throughout western Europe, provided the post-1968 generation of left-wing intellectuals – the ideological architects of today's social-justice movements that we have examined in this book – a false sense of security. They could call for revolution, expecting a more benign West to emerge if their dreams of social upheaval ever materialised. Indeed, the desire among so-called progressives to undermine the West's sense of itself, to reduce its power, deconstruct its narratives, challenge its philosophy and overthrow its institutional order is an impulse that, ironically, was under-pinned by a more confident and assured Western hegemony that is now waning and under great strain.

In the present context, the West is assailed by a cycle of rising domestic illiberalism and reaction deepening division and resentment. These tectonic shifts will realign winners and losers in the new dispensation. These shifts may unleash much darker movements that will also adopt the language of grievance and hatred but whose balance of power will likely outmatch our enlightened woke priests, that ultimately rely on the goodwill and patience of the very people they so despise. Internationally, the post-war liberal order is in deep flux, with powerful authoritarian 'civilisational-states' already freighting millions of souls into 're-education' camps or conducting their own 'special military operations'.

Our future has yet to be made and will be shaped by the choices we make today. As the world returns to a state of great power competition and the West heads further down a path of philosophical deconstruction and decolonisation, we must be careful what we wish for. Failure to grasp the importance of this means that the precious flame of freedom may be fully extinguished. It remains to be seen whether we still have the will to blow it alight again.

# Notes

## Introduction

1 *Independent.* 'Biden Divides Opinion as Comments Comparing Deaths of MLK and George Floyd Resurface', 18 January 2022.

2 United States Mission to the United Nations. 'Remarks by Ambassador Linda Thomas-Greenfield at the 30th Annual Summit of the National Action Network', 14 April 2021.

3 The White House. 'Advancing Equity and Racial Justice Through the Federal Government'. https://www.whitehouse.gov/equity/.

4 Task Force One Navy, https://media.defense.gov/2021/Jan/26 /2002570959/-1/-1/1/TASK%20FORCE%20ONE%20NAVY%20 FINAL%20REPORT.PDF

5 Benson, Dzifa. 'Claudia Rankine: "We Are inside a Culture That's Dedicated to Whiteness"', 6 May 2022. https://www.ft .com/content/1353904c-affa-4bdc-9b0b-14bf5a7eb475; See also Brownlee, Dana. 'Avoiding Terms Like "White Privilege" Is A Horrible Anti-Racism Strategy. Here's Why'. Forbes. https:// www.forbes.com/sites/danabrownlee/2022/08/25/avoiding-ter ms-like-white-privilege-is-a-horrible-anti-racism-strategyheres -why/.

6 'The Bias of "Professionalism" Standards (SSIR)'. https:// ssir.org/articles/entry/the_bias_of_professionalism_standards;

See also Judy Blair. 'White Supremacy Culture in a Pandemic', 16 April 2020. https://judy-blair.com/2020/04/16/white-supremacy-culture-in-a-pandemic/; Hoyle, Ben. 'Focusing on the Correct Answer in Maths "Is Racist"'. https://www.th etimes.co.uk/article/focusing-on-the-correct-answer-in-maths -is-racist-96gcztfs2.

7  Kerber, Ross, Jessica DiNapoli and Jessica DiNapoli. 'BlackRock Adds Diversity Target for US Boardrooms'. *Reuters*, 18 December 2021; see also Fortune. 'Is Your CEO an Anti-Racist?'. https://for tune.com/2022/09/09/next-street-managing-partner-says-c-sui te-needs-anti-racist-training-for-equity-commitments/.

8  United States Mission to the United Nations. 'Remarks by Ambassador Linda Thomas-Greenfield at the 30th Annual Summit of the National Action Network', 14 April 2021.

9  BBC News. 'Black Lives Matter Protests Held across England', 20 June 2020; McDonald, Henry. 'C of E Should Rethink Portrayal of Jesus as White, Welby Says'. *Guardian*, 26 June 2020, Karim, Fariha. 'Rural Britain Is Racist, Says Countryfile Presenter Ellie Harrison', https://www.thetimes.co.uk/article/rural-britain-is -racist-says-countryfile-presenter-ellie-harrison-wpk0lc7gn; on museums see Museums Association. 'Decolonising-Museums – Campaigns'. https://www.museumsassociation.org/campaig ns/decolonising-museums/; on the National Trust see National Trust. 'Addressing Our Histories of Colonialism and Historic Slavery'. https://www.nationaltrust.org.uk/features/addressing -the-histories-of-slavery-and-colonialism-at-the-national-trust.

10  *Times of India*. '35 Cops Injured in Further London Violence as Gandhi Statue Defaced', 9 June 2020.

11  Areo. 'Olúfẹ́mi Táíwò's "Against Decolonisation"', 17 June 2022; Táíwò, Olúfẹ́mi. *Against Decolonisation: Taking African Agency Seriously*. Hurst Publishers, 2022.

12  'Hidden in Plain Sight: Racism, White Supremacy, and Far-Right Militancy in Law Enforcement | Brennan Center for Justice'. https://www.brennancenter.org/our-work/research-reports/hid

den-plain-sight-racism-white-supremacy-and-far-right-militancy-law.

13  *Washington Post*. 'Fatal Force: Police Shootings Database'; See also 'CDE: Expanded Homicide Data'. https://cde.ucr.cjis.gov/LATEST/webapp/#/pages/homefor data.

14  'How Informed are Americans about Race and Policing?' Research Report: CUPES-007 | 20 February 2021, https://www.skeptic.com/research-center/reports/Research-Report-CUPES-007.pdf.

15  Mac Donald, Heather. 'Opinion | The Myth of Systemic Police Racism'. *Wall Street Journal*, 2 June 2020.

16  US Department of Justice Office, Criminal Victimization, 2021. September 2022, p. 10. https://bjs.ojp.gov/content/pub/pdf/cv21.pdf.

17  'CDE'. https://cde.ucr.cjis.gov/LATEST/webapp/#/pages/explorer/crime/crime-trend.

18  Fridel, Emma E., Keller G. Sheppard and Gregory M. Zimmerman. 'Integrating the Literature on Police Use of Deadly Force and Police Lethal Victimization: How Does Place Impact Fatal Police–Citizen Encounters?' *Journal of Quantitative Criminology* 36 (4) (December 2020): 968.

19  FBI. 'Table 42'. https://ucr.fbi.gov/leoka/2019/tables/table-42.xls.

20  Shjarback, John A. and Justin Nix. 'Considering Violence against Police by Citizen Race/Ethnicity to Contextualize Representation in Officer-Involved Shootings'. *Journal of Criminal Justice* 66 (1 January 2020).

21  Ibid., p. 8.

22  Worrall, John L., Stephen A. Bishopp, Scott C. Zinser, Andrew P. Wheeler and Scott W. Phillips. 'Exploring Bias in Police Shooting Decisions With Real Shoot/Don't Shoot Cases'. *Crime and Delinquency* 64 (9) (1 August 2018). For an extended survey of the literature on American policing and race see Brown, Robert A. and James Frank. 'Race and Officer Decision Making: Examining Differences in Arrest Outcomes between Black

and White Officers'. *Justice Quarterly* 23 (1) (1 March 2006): 96–126; Shane, Jon M., Brian Lawton and Zoë Swenson. 'The Prevalence of Fatal Police Shootings by US Police, 2015–2016: Patterns and Answers from a New Data Set'. *Journal of Criminal Justice* 52 (1 September 2017): 101–11; for a meta-analysis, see Oramas Mora, Daniela, William Terrill, and Jacob Foster. 'A Decade of Police Use of Deadly Force Research (2011–2020)'. *Homicide Studies*, 17 October 2022; Johnson, David J., Trevor Tress, Nicole Burkel, Carley Taylor and Joseph Cesario. 'Officer Characteristics and Racial Disparities in Fatal Officer-Involved Shootings'. *Proceedings of the National Academy of Sciences* 116 (32) (6 August 2019): 15877–82.

23  *Tablet Magazine.* 'Woke Terms and Media Racism Statistics', 5 August 2020.

24  Zraick, Karen. 'Dallas Officers Pinned Tony Timpa and Joked During Fatal Encounter, Video Shows'. *New York Times*, 1 August 2019.

25  Cramer, Maria. 'Video Appears to Show Death of California Man Held Down by Police'. *New York Times*, 17 March 2022.

26  FBI. 'Offenders'. https://ucr.fbi.gov/hate-crime/2019/topic-pa ges/offenders.

27  'CDE: Hate Crime'. https://crime-data-explorer.fr.cloud.gov/pa ges/explorer/crime/hate-crime.

28  Rozado, David. 'The Increasing Prominence of Prejudice and Social Justice Rhetoric in UK News Media'. Substack newsletter. *Rozado's Visual Analytics* (blog), 2 August 2022. https:// davidrozado.substack.com/p/tipopsjriuknm; see also 'Themes in Academic Literature: Prejudice and Social Justice by David Rozado  |  NAS'. https://www.nas.org/academic-questions/35 /2/themes-in-academic-literature-prejudice-and-social-justice.

29  'Discrimination in the European Union – September 2019 – Eurobarometer Survey'.

30  'Ethnic Group – Census Maps, ONS'. https://www.ons.gov.uk /census/maps/choropleth/identity/ethnic-group/ethnic-group -tb-20b/asian-asian-british-or-asian-welsh-bangladeshi.

31  *Economist.* 'Britain's Mixed-Race Population Blurs the Lines of Identity Politics', 3 October 2020. https://www.economist.com /britain/2020/10/03/britains-mixed-race-population-blurs-the -lines-of-identity-politics.

32  European Union Agency for Fundamental Rights. 'Fundamental Rights Report 2016', 28 April 2016. https://fra.europa.eu/en/pub lication/2016/fundamental-rights-report-2016.

33  European Union Agency for Fundamental Rights. 'Survey on Minorities and Discrimination in EU (2016)', 4 December 2017.

34  On data on UK Higher Education see 'Widening Participation in Higher Education, Academic Year 2019/20'. https://explore -education-statistics.service.gov.uk/find-statistics/widening-par ticipation-in-higher-education#dataBlock-b4f0a577-b45a-420d -a148-08d821b65a1f-tables.

35  'Widening Participation in Higher Education, Academic Year 2019/20'.https://explore-education-statistics.service.gov.uk/find -statistics/widening-participation-in-higher-education.

36  Although the terms BME and BAME have recently been aban-doned by the government, no alternative terminology has been proposed. Given that they are still widely used in discussions about race and equality, we have continued to employ them throughout this book.

37  'Ethnicity | University of Oxford'. https://www.ox.ac.uk/about /facts-and-figures/admissions-statistics/undergraduate-studen ts/current/ethnicity.

38  On ethnic pay gaps see 'Ethnicity Pay Gaps – Office for National Statistics'; see also 'Earnings and Working Hours – Office for National Statistics'.

39  '"Forgotten" White Working-Class Pupils Let down by Decades of Neglect, MPs Say – Committees – UK Parliament'. https:// committees.parliament.uk/committee/203/education-committ ee/news/156024/forgotten-white-workingclass-pupils-let-down -by-decades-of-neglect-mps-say/.

40  Ibid.

41  GOV.UK. 'Why Do People Come to the UK? To Work?' https:// www.gov.uk/government/statistics/immigration-statistics-ye ar-ending-september-2021/why-do-people-come-to-the-uk-to -work.

42  GOV.UK. 'Summary of Latest Statistics'. https://www.gov.uk /government/statistics/immigration-statistics-year-ending-de cember-2021/summary-of-latest-statistics.

43  *Financial Times.* 'Britain Is Now a High-Immigration Country and Most Are Fine with That', 12 May 2022.

44  College of Policing. 'Police Race Action Plan Published'. June 2022.

45  'Confidence in the Local Police'. https://www.ethnicity-facts-fi gures.service.gov.uk/crime-justice-and-the-law/policing/confi dence-in-the-local-police/latest.

46  'Themes in Academic Literature: Prejudice and Social Justice by David Rozado | NAS'. https://www.nas.org/academic-questions /35/2/themes-in-academic-literature-prejudice-and-social-justi ce.

## 1  Identity politics, decolonisation and social theory

1  'Long Live the Victory of People's War!' https://www.marxis ts.org/reference/archive/lin-biao/1965/09/peoples_war/ch07 .htm.

2  Sartre in Fanon, Frantz. *The Wretched of the Earth.* Grove Press, 1968, p. 22; for an introduction see Gordon, Lewis R. *What Fanon Said: A Philosophical Introduction to His Life and Thought.* Fordham University Press, 2015; Bulhan, Hussein Abdilahi. *Frantz Fanon and the Psychology of Oppression.* Springer Science & Business Media, 2004.

3  For the classic statement of the dependency theory school, see Frank, A. G. (1966) 'The Development of Underdevelopment', *Monthly Review* 18 (4): 17–31; see also Frank, Andre Gunder, Barry Gills and Barry K. Gills. *The World System: Five Hundred Years Or Five Thousand?* Psychology Press, 1993; Batou, Jean. *Between Development and Underdevelopment: The Precocious*

*Attempts at Industrialization of the Periphery, 1800-1870.* Librairie Droz, 1991; Falola, Toyin and Jessica Achberger. *The Political Economy of Development and Underdevelopment in Africa.* Routledge, 2015.

4  Wallerstein, Immanuel. *The Modern World-System I: Capitalist Agriculture and the Origins of the European World-Economy in the Sixteenth Century* (1st edn). University of California Press, 2011; see also Wallerstein, Immanuel. *The Modern World-System III: The Second Era of Great Expansion of the Capitalist World-Economy, 1730s–1840s, With a New Prologue.* University of California Press, 2011; Wallerstein, Immanuel Maurice and Senior Researcher Immanuel Wallerstein. *World-Systems Analysis: An Introduction.* Duke University Press, 2004.

5  Andrews, Kehinde. *The New Age of Empire: How Racism and Colonialism Still Rule the World.* Allen Lane, Penguin Books, 2021; for more in this genre see Andrews, Kehinde. *Empire 2.0.* Public Affairs, 2020; Sanghera, Sathnam. *Empireland: How Imperialism Has Shaped Modern Britain.* Penguin UK, 2021; Gopal, Priyamvada. *Insurgent Empire: Anticolonial Resistance and British Dissent.* Verso Books, 2019.

6  PBS NewsHour. 'How the West Got Rich and Modern Capitalism Was Born', 13 February 2015.

7  Dikötter, Frank. *The Cultural Revolution: A People's History, 1962–1976.* Bloomsbury Publishing, 2016; see also his excellent Dikötter, Frank. *The Tragedy of Liberation: A History of the Chinese Revolution 1945-1957.* A&C Black, 2013.

8  Lindsay, James. *Race Marxism: The Truth About Critical Race Theory and Praxis.* Amazon Digital Services LLC – KDP Print US, 2022.

9  Marcuse, Herbert. *An Essay on Liberation.* Beacon Press, 1971, pp.15–16.

10  Ibid., pp. 57–8.

11  Althusser, Louis. *On Ideology.* Verso Books, 2020; see also Lewis, William S. *Louis Althusser and the Traditions of French*

*Marxism*. Lexington Books, 2005; Althusser, Louis. *On Ideology*. Verso Books, 2020.

12 See the masterful early work in this genre: Jameson, Fredric. *Postmodernism: Or, the Cultural Logic of Late Capitalism*. Reprint edn. London: Verso Books, 1992; for a critical introduction see Kellner, D. and S. Homer. *Fredric Jameson: A Critical Reader*. Springer, 2004.

13 Lyotard, Jean-Francois. *The Postmodern Condition: A Report on Knowledge*. Manchester: Manchester University Press, 1984; for an attempt to reconcile intersectionality and Marxism see Bohrer, Ashley J. *Marxism and Intersectionality: Race, Gender, Class and Sexuality under Contemporary Capitalism*. Bielefeld: Transcript Verlag, 2019.

14 Afary, Janet and Kevin B. Anderson. *Foucault and the Iranian Revolution: Gender and the Seductions of Islamism*. Annotated edition. Chicago: University of Chicago Press, 2005; see also Ghamari-Tabrizi, Behrooz. *Foucault in Iran: Islamic Revolution after the Enlightenment*. University of Minnesota Press, 2016.

15 Foucault, Michel. *The Order of Things*. London: Routledge, 2001, p. 168; see also Foucault, Michel. *Discipline and Punish: The Birth of the Prison*. Vintage Books, 1995; for a semi biographical work, see the excellent Miller, James and Jim Miller. *The Passion of Michel Foucault*. Harvard University Press, 2000.

16 Hutcheon, Linda. '"Circling the Downspout of Empire": Post-Colonialism and Postmodernism', 1989, p. 155. https://tspace.library.utoronto.ca/handle/1807/10262; see also her *The Politics of Postmodernism*. Routledge, 2003.

17 Said, Edward W. 'Orientalism', in *Social Theory Re-Wired* (2nd edn). Routledge, 2016, p. 3; see also Kennedy, Valerie. *Edward Said: A Critical Introduction*. Wiley, 2000; Said, Edward W. *Culture and Imperialism*. Knopf, 1993; for an excellent introduction to Said see Ashcroft, Bill and Pal Ahluwalia. *Edward Said*. Routledge, 2008.

18 Bhambra, Gurminder K. 'Postcolonial and Decolonial Dialogues'. *Postcolonial Studies* 17 (2) (3 April 2014): 115–21, p. 118;

For an extended discussion see her *Rethinking Modernity: Postcolonialism and the Sociological Imagination*. Springer, 2007.

19  'Rutazibwa, Olivia U. and Robbie Shilliam. *Routledge Handbook of Postcolonial Politics*. Routledge, 2018, p. 19; see also Shilliam, Robbie. *Decolonizing Politics: An Introduction*. John Wiley & Sons, 2021.

20  Quijano, Aníbal. 'Coloniality of Power and Eurocentrism in Latin America'. *International Sociology* 15 (2) (1 June 2000): 215–32, p. 222; see also Davies, Carole Boyce, Meredith Gadsby, Charles F. Peterson and Henrietta Williams. *Decolonizing the Academy: African Diaspora Studies*. Africa World Press, 2003.

21  Legatum Institute. 'Is Academic Freedom Under Threat?' https://li.com/reports/is-academic-freedom-under-threat/.

22  Choat, Simon. 'Decolonising the Political Theory Curriculum'. *Politics* 41 (3) (1 August 2021): 404–20.

23  Bhambra, Gurminder K., Dalia Gebrial and Kerem Nişancıoğlu, eds. *Decolonising the University*. Pluto Press, 2018, p. 5.

24  Shilliam, Robbie, in Bhambra, Gurminder K., Dalia Gebrial and Kerem Nişancıoğlu, eds. *Decolonising the University*. Pluto Press, 2018, p. 59.

25  Guess, Teresa J. 'The Social Construction of Whiteness: Racism by Intent, Racism by Consequence'. *Critical Sociology* 32 (4) (1 July 2006): 649–73; see also Michael, Lucy and Samantha Schulz. *Unsettling Whiteness*. Brill, 2019; Turner, Sarah E. and Sarah Nilsen. *The Myth of Colorblindness: Race and Ethnicity in American Cinema*. Springer Nature, 2019.

26  Guess, Teresa J. 'The Social Construction of Whiteness: Racism by Intent, Racism by Consequence'. *Critical Sociology* 32 (4) (1 July 2006): 649–73, p. 664.

27  Ibid., p. 656.

28  For an interesting critique of whiteness studies see Niemonen, Jack. 'Public Sociology or Partisan Sociology? The Curious Case of Whiteness Studies'. *American Sociologist* 41 (1) (1 March 2010): 48–81.

29  Applebaum, Barbara. *Being White, Being Good: White Complicity, White Moral Responsibility, and Social Justice Pedagogy.* Lexington Books, 2010, p. 179.
30  Andrews, Kehinde. 'The Psychosis of Whiteness: The Celluloid Hallucinations of Amazing Grace and Belle'. *Journal of Black Studies* 47 (5) (1 July 2016): 435–53.
31  DiAngelo, Robin. *White Fragility: Why It's So Hard for White People to Talk About Racism.* Penguin UK, 2019, p. 129.
32  Maldonado-Torres, Nelson, Rafael Vizcaíno, Jasmine Wallace and Jeong Eun Annabel We. 'Decolonising Philosophy', in *Decolonising the University*, edited by Gurminder K. Bhambra, Dalia Gebrial and Kerem Nişancıoğlu, 4–90. London: Pluto Press, 2018, pp. 64–5.
33  Sofia Akel, 'What Decolonising The Curriculum Really Means'. *EachOther* (blog), 14 August 2020. https://eachother.org.uk/de colonising-the-curriculum-what-it-really-means/; see also Jones, Steven. *Universities Under Fire: Hostile Discourses and Integrity Deficits in Higher Education.* Springer Nature, 2022.

## 2  Racism on campus

1  'Universities Oblivious to Scale of Racial Abuse on Campus | Equality and Human Rights Commission'. https://www.equality humanrights.com/en/our-work/news/universities-oblivious-sca le-racial-abuse-campus.
2  Batty, David. 'Universities Failing to Address Thousands of Racist Incidents'. *Guardian*, 23 October 2019.
3  UCU 'In the News: 11 October'. https://www.ucu.org.uk/article /10357/In-the-news-11-October.
4  Ibid.
5  'Racial Harassment Inquiry: Survey of University Students | Equality and Human Rights Commission'.
6  Batty, David. 'Universities Failing to Address Thousands of Racist Incidents'. *Guardian*, 23 October 2019.
7  'Tackling Racial Harassment: Universities Challenged'. Equality and Human Rights Commission.

8 Ibid., p. 10.
9 UUK. 'Tackling Racial Harassment in Higher Education'.
10 Ibid., pp. 4–5.
11 Ibid.
12 David Richardson, WonkHE. 'Tackling Racial Harassment in Higher Education'. October 2020. https://wonkhe.com/blogs/tackling-racial-harassment-in-higher-education/.
13 Debbie McVitty, WonkHE. 'Acknowledging Institutional Racism Is Only the First Step'. https://wonkhe.com/blogs/acknowledging-institutional-racism-is-only-the-first-step/.
14 'Tackling Racial Harassment in Higher Education', p. 41.
15 Ibid.
16 'Home | Advance HE'. https://www.advance-he.ac.uk/.
17 'Race Equality Charter | Advance HE'. https://www.advance-he.ac.uk/equality-charters/race-equality-charter.
18 See Introduction, note 36.
19 'Appendix 1: Race Equality Charter (REC) Review Survey' in Freya Douglas Oloyede, Ashlee Christoffersen and Tinu Cornish, *Race Equality Charter Review*, pp. 14, 99. https://s3.eu-west-2.amazonaws.com/assets.creode.advancehe-document-manager/documents/advance-he/AdvHE_REC_Review_Appendices_16 18582927.pdf.
20 Appendix 1: Race Equality Charter (REC) Review Survey' in Freya Douglas Oloyede, Ashlee Christoffersen and Tinu Cornish, *Race Equality Charter Review*, pp. 16, 101. https://s3.eu-west-2.amazonaws.com/assets.creode.advancehe-document-manager/documents/advance-he/AdvHE_REC_Review_Appendices_1618582 927.pdf
21 Universities UK. 'Black, Asian and Minority Ethnic Student Attainment at UK Universities: Closing the Gap'.
22 'SOAS Director Co-Leads Initiative to Close BAME Attainment Gap in Universities | SOAS University of London'. https://www.soas.ac.uk/news/newsitem140450.html.
23 'Universities Acting to Close BAME Student Attainment Gap @ NUS'.

24 Universities UK. 'Black, Asian and Minority Ethnic Student Attainment at UK Universities: Closing the Gap'.

25 Murray, Seb. '"Real Change Is Needed": Addressing the BAME Postgrad Attainment Gap'. *Guardian*, 16 February 2021.

26 Sussex, University of. '#BlackLivesMatter'. The University of Sussex. https://www.sussex.ac.uk/broadcast/read/52197.

27 Akinbosede, Daniel. 'The BAME Attainment Gap Is Not the Fault of BAME Students'. *Times Higher Education (THE)*, 5 December 2019.

28 Goldsmiths, University of London. 'Awarding Gap (Attainment Gap)'. https://www.gold.ac.uk/race-justice/awarding-gap/.

29 'Why Is My Curriculum White? – Decolonising the Academy @ NUS Connect'. https://www.nusconnect.org.uk/articles/why-is-my-curriculum-white-decolonising-the-academy.

30 Universities UK. 'Data'. 2022 . https://www.universitiesuk.ac.uk/what-we-do/policy-and-research/publications/features/closingthegap-three-years/data.

31 Universities UK. 'Racially Diverse and Inclusive Communities'. 2022. https://www.universitiesuk.ac.uk/what-we-do/policy-and-research/publications/features/closingthegap-three-years/racially-diverse-and-inclusive.

32 Universities UK. 'Black, Asian and Minority Ethnic Student Attainment at UK Universities: Closing the Gap'.

33 'Infographic: The Story of the Race Equality Charter | Advance HE'. https://www.advance-he.ac.uk/news-and-views/infographic-story-race-equality-charter.

34 'Developing Solutions to Racial Inequalities, It Is Important That They Are Aimed at Achieving Long-Term Institutional Culture Change" Whilst "Avoiding a Deficit Model Where Solutions Are Aimed at Changing the Individual" – Google Search'. http://tinyurl.com/2y5yd9zy.

35 University, Keele. 'Keele Decolonising the Curriculum Network'. Keele University.

36 'KCLSU and KCL Agreement Signing 2019'. https://www.kclsu
.org/news/article/6015/KCLSU-and-KCL-Agreement-Signing
-2019/.

37 'Decolonising    SOAS'.    https://blogs.soas.ac.uk/decolonisings
oas/.

38 Universities UK. 'Tackling Racial Harassment in Higher
Education'. Case Studies, p. 13.

39 Innovating Pedagogy 2019 – Exploring new forms of teaching,
learning and assessment, to guide educators and policy makers,
Open University Innovation Report 7 https://www.open.edu
/openlearn/ocw/pluginfile.php/2569410/mod_resource/content
/1/innovating-pedagogy-2019.pdf.

40 *Times Higher Education* (*THE*). 'London University Develops
"Indigenous-Led" Teaching and Research', 23 May 2019.

41 Centre for Indigenous and Settler Colonial Studies. 'Centre for
Indigenous and Settler Colonial Studies – Research at Kent'.

42 BBC News. 'Anger at University of Leicester's "Decolonised
Curriculum" Plans', 4 February 2021.

43 'Decolonisation: Race Equality and Higher Education | Social
Worlds in 100 Objects, Themes and Ideas | University of
Leicester'.    https://le.ac.uk/social-worlds/all-articles/decolonis
ation.

44 'Decolonise Sociology @ Cambridge'.

45 Gerstmann, Evan. '"White Lives Don't Matter," Academic
Freedom and Freedom Of Speech'. *Forbes*.

46 'A Commitment to Change, Part II – Cambridge University
Museums'.    https://www.museums.cam.ac.uk/blog/2020/07/22
/a-commitment-to-change-part-ii/; 'Open Letter to Cambridge
Museums', pp. 6–8. https://docs.google.com/document/d/1o
MKWON0_pgPulTKYW8q5Nklo74JCwUwPHEvVs2WvLVM
/edit#.

47 Carr, Caitlin. 'Reclassification', 9 *West Road*, 2020, p. 38. https://
www.english.cam.ac.uk/alumni/newsletter/9westroad19.pdf
?utm_source=alumniemail&utm_campaign=alumni&utm_med
ium=email&redirect=aHR0cHM6Ly93d3cuZW5nbGlzaC5jYW

0uYWMudWsvYWx1bW5pL25ld3NsZXR0ZXIvOXdlc3Ryb
2FkMTkucGRmP3V0bV9zb3VyY2U9YWx1bW5pZW1ha
WwmdXRtX2NhbXBhaWduPWFsdW1uaSZ1dG1fbWVkaXVt
PWVtYWls.

48  Bach, Mel. 'Cambridge University Libraries Decolonisation
Working Group'. Text, 29 October 2020. https://www.lib.cam
.ac.uk/about-library/diversifying-collections-and-practices/cam
bridge-university-libraries-decolonisation.

49  Turner, Camilla. 'Cambridge Museum to Explain "Whiteness"
of its Sculptures under Anti-Racism Campaign'. *Telegraph*,
22 August 2021.

50  Thompson, N. M. 'Open Letter on Anti-Racism: A Response
from the Faculty Board of Classics'. Text, 16 July 2021. https://
www.classics.cam.ac.uk/news/open-letter-anti-racism-response
-faculty-board-classics.

51  Turner, Camilla. 'Cambridge Museum to Explain "Whiteness"
of Its Sculptures under Anti-Racism Campaign'. *Telegraph*,
22 August 2021.

52  Hillman, Nick. 'Views on Decolonising the Curriculum Depend
on How Changes Are Presented'. HEPI, 19 July 2021.

53  *Independent*. 'Less than a Quarter of People Agree with
Decolonising Curriculum, Poll Suggests'.

54  Ibid.

55  See Rollock, Nicola. 'Unspoken Rules of Engagement: Navigating
Racial Microaggressions in the Academic Terrain'. *International
Journal of Qualitative Studies in Education* 25 (5) (1 August 2012):
517–32. EHRC, Tackling Racial Harassment in universities.

56  'Equality Act Guidance | Equality and Human Rights
Commission'. https://www.equalityhumanrights.com/en/advice
-and-guidance/equality-act-guidance.

57  King's Race Equality Action Plan Building an antiracist university 2020–2024. https://www.kcl.ac.uk/hr/diversity/assets/docu
ments/king's-race-equality-action-plan-2020-2024.pdf.

58  Liverpool University, Equality Framework Implementation
Action Plan 2016–2026. https://www.liverpool.ac.uk/media/liva

cuk/hr/diversityandequality/policiesandactionplans/Equality,Fr
amework,Implementation,Action,Plan,Web.pdf.

59 'University Commits to Tackling Racial Harassment in UK
Higher Education | Solent University'. https://www.solent.ac.uk
/news/university-commits-to-tackling-racial-harassment-in-uk
-higher-education.

60 BBC News. 'Sheffield Students Paid to Tackle Racist Language
on Campus', 14 January 2020.

61 'Common Racial Microaggressions'. The University of Edinburgh.
https://www.ed.ac.uk/equality-diversity/students/microaggres
sions/what-are-microaggressions.

62 'Microaggressions – What You Should Know'. Faculty of
Engineering, Imperial College London'.

63 Woolcock, Nicola. Editor, Education. 'St Andrew's University
Sets Bias Test for Entry', sec. news. https://www.thetimes.co.uk
/article/pass-bias-test-to-enter-st-andrews-rgcvcglx3.

## 3  Moral panic and illiberalism in universities

1 'Ethnic Group – Census Maps, ONS'. https://www.ons.gov.uk
/census/maps/choropleth/identity/ethnic-group/ethnic-group
-tb-20b/asian-asian-british-or-asian-welsh-bangladeshi.

2 'Tackling Racial Harassment: Universities Challenged'. Equality
and Human Rights Commission, p. 10.

3 Racial Harassment Inquiry: Survey of University Students |
Equality and Human Rights Commission (no date). Available
at: https://www.equalityhumanrights.com/en/publication-down
load/racial-harassment-inquiry-survey-university-students-0.

4 Harford, Tim. 'Down with Mathiness!' *Financial Times*, 5 June
2015.

5 'Racial Harassment Inquiry: Survey of Universities | Equality and
Human Rights Commission', p. 21.

6 See for example the '100 Black Women Professors NOW'.
https://www.whenequality.org/100.

7 'Race Equality Charter | Advance HE'. https://www.advance-he
.ac.uk/equality-charters/race-equality-charter.

8  WonkHE. 'Supporting Evidence-Based Action on Racial Inequality Is Not "Wokery"'.

9  'Equality in Higher Education: Statistical Report 2021 | Advance HE', p. 130.

10  Ibid., pp. 131–2.

11  Ibid., p. 132.

12  Ibid., p. 126.

13  Ibid., p. 127.

14  'Ethnicity | University of Oxford'. https://www.ox.ac.uk/about /facts-and-figures/admissions-statistics/undergraduate-studen ts/current/ethnicity.

15  Cineas, Fabiola. 'Is Meritocracy a Myth?' *Vox*, 2 April 2021; Anderson, Melinda D. 'What Happens When Poor Kids Are Taught Society Is Fair'. *Atlantic*, 27 July 2017.

16  'Table 26 – UK Domiciled First Degree Qualifiers by Classification of First Degree, Religious Belief, Sex, Age Group, Disability Marker and Ethnicity Marker 2014/15 to 2020/21 | HESA'. https://www.hesa.ac.uk/data-and-analysis/students/table-26.

17  Office for Students, Student Outcomes Summary Data. https:// www.officeforstudents.org.uk/media/447bf92c-24d0-4b9f-9007 -b7a787320585/student-outcomes-summary-data-march2019 .xlsx.

18  Ibid.

19  'Temporary Exclusions – GOV.UK Ethnicity Facts and Figures'. https://www.ethnicity-facts-figures.service.gov.uk/education-sk ills-and-training/absence-and-exclusions/pupil-exclusions/la test.

20  'Widening Participation in Higher Education, Academic Year 2019/20'. https://explore-education-statistics.service.gov.uk /find-statistics/widening-participation-in-higher-education.

21  Owolade, Tomiwa. 'Obsession with Race Tells Only Half a Story', https://www.thetimes.co.uk/article/obsession-with-race -tells-only-half-a-story-f7vm8j3n6.

22  BBC News. 'NUS President Dismissed over Anti-Semitism Claims', 1 November 2022.

23 Mitchell, Travis. '6. Jewish Educational Attainment'. *Pew Research Center's Religion & Public Life Project* (blog), 13 December 2016.

24 'Jewish Nobel Prize Winners'. http://www.jinfo.org/Nobel_Pri zes.html?utm_source=substack&utm_medium=email.

25 *Independent*. 'Private School Pupils Likely to "Elbow out" State Students in Scramble for University Places, Experts Warn', 10 August 2021.

26 Advance HE. Students statistical report 2021.

27 'Undergraduate Degree Results'. https://www.ethnicity-facts-fi gures.service.gov.uk/education-skills-and-training/higher-educ ation/undergraduate-degree-results/latest.

28 BBC News. 'Five Charts That Tell the Story of Diversity in UK Universities', 23 May 2018.

29 Sue, Derald Wing, Christina M. Capodilupo, Gina C. Torino, Jennifer M. Bucceri, Aisha M. B. Holder, Kevin L. Nadal and Marta Esquilin. 'Racial Microaggressions in Everyday Life: Implications for Clinical Practice'. *American Psychologist* 62 (4) (June 2007): 271–86.; for useful critiques of microaggression theory see Lilienfeld, Scott O. 'Microaggressions: Strong Claims, Inadequate Evidence'. *Perspectives on Psychological Science* 12 (1) (1 January 2017): 138–69. See also Campbell, Bradley and Jason Manning. 'Microaggression and Moral Cultures'. *Comparative Sociology* 13 (6) (30 January 2014): 692–726; in the US context see Friedersdorf, Conor. 'Microaggressions and the Rise of Victimhood Culture'. *Atlantic*, 11 September 2015.

30 'Constantine, M. G. and Sue, D. W. (2007). Perceptions of racial microaggressions among black supervisees in cross-racial dyads. *Journal of Counseling Psychology, 54*(2), 142–53.

31 Webber, Ashleigh. 'UK Leads the World in D&I Roles'. *Personnel Today* (blog), 10 September 2020. https://www.personneltoday .com/hr/surge-in-demand-for-di-roles-in-past-five-years/.

32 Campbell, Bradley and Jason Manning. 'Microaggression and Moral Cultures'. *Comparative Sociology* 13 (6) (30 January 2014): 692–726.

33 'Tackling Racial Harassment in Higher Education'. November 2020. universitiesuk.ac.uk Executive summary, p. 11. https://www.universitiesuk.ac.uk/sites/default/files/uploads/Reports/tackling-racial-harassment-in-higher-education-exec.pdf.

34 'Tackling Racial Harassment: Universities Challenged | Equality and Human Rights Commission', p. 30.

35 Hockaday, James. 'Cambridge Vice-Chancellor Admits List of "Micro-Aggressions" Was a Mistake'. Metro (blog), 28 May 2021.

36 Advance HE. Microaggressions. Call it Racism. https://www.uws.ac.uk/media/7317/advance-he-microaggressions.pdf.

37 Kandola, Binna. *Racism at Work: The Danger of Indifference.* Pearn Kandola Publishing, 2018.

38 'The Modern Form of Racism: Micro-Incivilities | Advance HE'. https://www.advance-he.ac.uk/news-and-views/modern-racism-micro-incivilities.

39 'The Forgotten: How White Working-Class Pupils Have Been Let Down, and How to Change It – Education Committee – House of Commons'. https://publications.parliament.uk/pa/cm5802/cmselect/cmeduc/85/8503.htm; see also BBC News. 'The "Taboo" about Who Doesn't Go to University', 26 September 2020.

40 ONS. 'Entry Rates into Higher Education'.

41 NEON. 'New Report Shows Differences in White Working Class Students Going to University by Higher Education Provider', 14 February 2019. https://www.educationopportunities.co.uk/news/new-report-shows-differences-in-white-working-class-students-going-to-university-by-higher-education-provider/.

42 'Ethnicity Pay Gaps in Britain – Office for National Statistics'. https://www.ons.gov.uk/employmentandlabourmarket/peopleinwork/earningsandworkinghours/articles/ethnicitypaygapsingreatbritain/2018.

43 BBC News. 'Why Do More Women than Men Go to University?', 18 August 2016.

44 'What Are HE Students' Progression Rates and Qualifications? | HESA'. https://www.hesa.ac.uk/data-and-analysis/students/outcomes.

## 4 History reclaimed

1 Delgado, Richard and Jean Stefancic, Critical Race Theory: An Introduction (3rd edn).

2 Black, Jeremy. *Imperial Legacies: The British Empire Around the World*. New York: Encounter Books, 2019, p. 11.

3 Rutazibwa, Olivia U. and Robbie Shilliam. *Routledge Handbook of Postcolonial Politics*. Routledge, 2018, p. 19.

4 Irfan, Lamia, Muzammil Quraishi, Mallory Schneuwly Purdie and Matthew Wilkinson. 'The Primacy of Ontology: A Philosophical Basis for Research on Religion in Prison'. *Journal of Critical Realism* 21 (2):1–25.

5 Sayer, Andrew. *Realism and Social Science*. 1st edn. London ; Thousand Oaks, Calif: SAGE Publications Ltd, 1999, p. 48.

6 McLaughlin, Mark. '"Haven for Bigots" Remark Deepens Campus Dispute', https://www.thetimes.co.uk/article/haven-for-bigots-remark-deepens-campus-dispute-7crd79d8l.

7 Stock, Kathleen. *Material Girls: Why Reality Matters for Feminism*. London: Fleet, 2022.

8 Afful, Adwoa A. and Rose Ricciardelli. 'Shaping the Online Fat Acceptance Movement: Talking about Body Image and Beauty Standards'. *Journal of Gender Studies* 24 (4) (4 July 2015): 453–72; Ravary, Amanda, Mark W. Baldwin and Jennifer A. Bartz. 'Shaping the Body Politic: Mass Media Fat-Shaming Affects Implicit Anti-Fat Attitudes'. *Personality and Social Psychology Bulletin* 45 (11) (November 2019): 1580–89.

9 Patomäki, Heikki. *After International Relations: Critical Realism and the (Re)Construction of World Politics*. 1st edn. London; New York: Routledge, 2001, p. 9.

10 For the classic articulation see Bhaskar, Roy. *A Realist Theory of Science*. Verso Books, 2008; see also the excellent Bhaskar, Roy. *The Possibility of Naturalism: A Philosophical Critique of the Contemporary Human Sciences*. Routledge, 2014. For a useful introduction see Sayer, Andrew. *Realism and Social Science*. SAGE, 2000.

11 Nordling, Linda. 'How Decolonization Could Reshape

South African Science'. *Nature* 554 (7691) (7 February 2018): 159–62.

12 Prescod-Weinstein, Chanda. 'Making Black Women Scientists under White Empiricism: The Racialization of Epistemology in Physics'. *Signs: Journal of Women in Culture and Society* 45 (2) (January 2020): 421–47.

13 QAA. Subject Benchmark Statement Mathematics, Statistics and Operational Research 5th edn. September 2022. https://www.qaa.ac.uk/docs/qaa/quality-code/sbs-mathematics-statistics-and-operational-research-consultation-22.pdf?sfvrsn=f3b9a581_4; for background see *Times Higher Education* (*THE*). 'Professors Say Decolonisation Agenda "Politicising" Maths Degrees', 7 November 2022.

14 Táíwò, Olúfẹ́mi. Against Decolonisation: Taking African Agency Seriously. Hurst Publishers, 2022.

15 Areo. 'Olúfẹ́mi Táíwò's "Against Decolonisation"', 17 June 2022. https://areomagazine.com/2022/06/17/olufemi-taiwos-against-decolonisation/.

16 Niemonen, J. (2010) 'Public Sociology or Partisan Sociology? The Curious Case of Whiteness Studies', *American Sociologist*, 41(1): 48–81.

17 Adekoya, Remi. 'The Truth about Elizabeth's Empire'. *UnHerd*, 12 September 2022.

18 *Economist*. 'African Kleptocrats Are Finding It Tougher to Stash Cash in the West'. 10 October, 2019.

19 *Punch* Newspapers. 'Nearly $600bn Stolen from Nigeria since Independence – Economist', 11 October 2019.

20 Adekoya, Remi. 'The Truth about Elizabeth's Empire'. *UnHerd*, 12 September 2022.

21 Christiaan Keulder, 'Africans See Growing Corruption, Poor Government Response, but Fear Retaliation if They Speak Out'. Afrobarometer Dispatch No. 4881.

22 African Youth Survey 2022, Ichikowitz Foundation; For more context see Ordu, Ivor Ichikowitz and Aloysius Uche. 'African Youth Survey Reveals Sustained Optimism and Shifting

Priorities'. *Brookings* (blog), 20 July 2022. https://www.brookings
.edu/podcast-episode/african-youth-survey-reveals-sustained
-optimism-and-shifting-priorities/.

23  *Economist.* 'Chinese Loans and Investment in Infrastructure
Have Been Huge'. https://www.economist.com/special-report
/2022/05/20/chinese-loans-and-investment-in-infrastructure
-have-been-huge.

24  Shepard, Wade. 'What China Is Really Up To In Africa'. *Forbes.*
https://www.forbes.com/sites/wadeshepard/2019/10/03/what
-china-is-really-up-to-in-africa/.

25  Wheatley, Paul. 'Geographical Notes on Some Commodities
Involved in Sung Maritime Trade'. *Journal of the Malayan
Branch of the Royal Asiatic Society* 32 (2) (186) (1959):
3–140.

26  Chaffee, John W., ed. 'Merchants of an Imperial Trade', in *The
Muslim Merchants of Premodern China: The History of a Maritime
Asian Trade Diaspora, 750–1400*, 12–50. New Approaches to
Asian History. Cambridge: Cambridge University Press, 2018.

27  Wyatt, Don J. *The Blacks of Premodern China*. University of
Pennsylvania Press, 2012.

28  Areo. 'The Forgotten History of African Slavery in China',
19 March 2021. https://areomagazine.com/2021/03/19/the-for
gotten-history-of-african-slavery-in-china/; see also Dikötter,
Frank. *The Discourse of Race in Modern China*. C. Hurst & Co.
Publishers, 1994.

29  Bruckner, Pascal. *The Tyranny of Guilt: An Essay on Western
Masochism*. Princeton University Press, 2010.

30  'Said, Edward W. *Culture and Imperialism*. Random House,
2014, pp. xxv–xxvi.

31  Puri, Samir. *The Great Imperial Hangover: How Empires Have
Shaped the World*. Atlantic Books, 2020, p. 14.

32  The Campus Learn, Share, Connect. 'Is It Possible to Decolonise
the Business Curriculum?', 11 August 2022. https://www.times
highereducation.com/campus/it-possible-decolonise-business
-curriculum.

33 'Slavery After 1807 – Ending Slavery | Historic England'. http://historicengland.org.uk/research/inclusive-heritage/the-slave-trade-and-abolition/sites-of-memory/ending-slavery/slavery-after-1807/; see also 'Slave Trade Act 1824'. Queen's Printer of Acts of Parliament. https://www.legislation.gov.uk/ukpga/Geo4/5/113/enacted.

34 United Nations. 'International Day for the Abolition of Slavery'. United Nations. United Nations. https://www.un.org/en/observances/slavery-abolition-day.

35 'Countries That Still Have Slavery 2022'. https://worldpopulationreview.com/country-rankings/countries-that-still-have-slavery.

36 Paliath, Shreehari. 'Income Inequality in India: Top 10% Upper Caste Households Own 60% Wealth'. *Business Standard India*, 14 January 2019.

37 BBC News. 'Caste Discrimination Law Faces Appalling Delays, Say Campaigners', 30 July 2013.

38 Pedalo. 'Descent-Based Slavery'. *Anti-Slavery International* (blog). https://www.antislavery.org/slavery-today/descent-based-slavery/.

39 On Haiti, see L'Ouverture, Toussaint. *The Haitian Revolution*. London: Verso, 2019; on the Abolitionist movement, Charles River. *Olaudah Equiano: The Life and Legacy of the Freed Slave Whose Autobiography Fuelled Britain's Abolitionist Movement*. CreateSpace Independent Publishing Platform, 2017.

40 *The Critic Magazine*. 'The Royal Navy in the Front Line against Slavery | Jeremy Black', 18 October 2020. https://thecritic.co.uk/the-royal-navy-in-the-front-line-against-slavery/; See also Sullivan, Anthony. *Britain's War Against the Slave Trade: The Operations of the Royal Navy's West Africa Squadron 1807-1867*. Frontline Books, 2020; Edwards, Bernard. *Royal Navy Versus the Slave Traders: Enforcing Abolition at Sea 1808–1898*. Pen & Sword Maritime, 2021.

41 'Chasing Freedom: The Royal Navy and the Suppression of the Transatlantic Slave Trade, an Exhibition Review'. https://arch

ives.history.ac.uk/1807commemorated/exhibitions/museums /chasing.html.

42  Hamilton, Keith and Patrick Salmon, eds, *Slavery, Diplomacy and Empire: Britain and the Suppression of the Slave Trade, 1807–1975* (Sussex Academic Press, 2009); See also Hugh Thomas, *The Slave Trade: A History of the Atlantic Slave Trade,* 1440-1870. Picador, 1997.

43  'BBC – Religions – Islam: Slavery in Islam'. https://www.bbc.co .uk/religion/religions/islam/history/slavery_1.shtml.

44  Laing, Stuart. *Tippu Tip: Ivory, Slavery and Discovery in the Scramble for Africa.* Surbiton, Surrey: Medina Publishing Ltd, 2017.

45  Sheriff, Abdul. *Slaves, Spices and Ivory in Zanzibar: Integration of an East African Commercial Empire into the World Economy, 1770–1873.* Ohio University Press, 1987.

46  Page, Melvin E. 'The Manyema Hordes of Tippu Tip: A Case Study in Social Stratification and the Slave Trade in Eastern Africa'. *International Journal of African Historical Studies* 7 (1) (1974): 69–84.

47  Fair, Laura. *Pastimes and Politics: Culture, Community, and Identity in Post-Abolition Urban Zanzibar, 1890–1945.* Ohio University Press, 2001, p. 12.

48  Boswell, Rosabelle. *Challenges to Identifying and Managing Intangible Cultural Heritage in Mauritius, Zanzibar and Seychelles.* African Books Collective, 2008, p. 26.

49  Lovejoy, Paul E. and Jan S. Hogendorn. *Slow Death for Slavery: The Course of Abolition in Northern Nigeria 1897–1936.* African Studies. Cambridge: Cambridge University Press, 1993, p. xiii.

50  Last, Murray. 'Slavery and the Slave Trade in the Sokoto Caliphate'. *Oxford Research Encyclopedia of African History,* 26 April 2021.

51  Salau, Mohammed Bashir. *Plantation Slavery in the Sokoto Caliphate: A Historical and Comparative Study (Rochester Studies in African History and the Diaspora): 80.* Rochester: University of Rochester Press, 2018, p. 29.

52  Azumah, J. & Azumah, J. A. (2001). *The Legacy of Arab–Islam in Africa: A Quest for Inter-Religious Dialogue.* Oneworld Publications Ltd, p. 161.

53  Davis, Robert C. *Christian Slaves, Muslim Masters: White Slavery in the Mediterranean, the Barbary Coast and Italy, 1500–1800.* London: Palgrave Macmillan, 2003.

54  Leiner, Frederick C. *The End of Barbary Terror: America's 1815 War against the Pirates of North Africa.* Oxford, New York: Oxford University Press, 2007, p. 15.

55  Capp, B. S. *British Slaves and Barbary Corsairs, 1580–1750.* Oxford: Oxford University Press, 2022.

56  Oborne, Peter. *The Fate of Abraham: Why the West Is Wrong about Islam.* London: Simon & Schuster UK, 2022.

57  Department of State. The Office of Electronic Information, Bureau of Public Affairs. 'Barbary Wars, 1801–1805 and 1815–1816'. Department of State. The Office of Electronic Information, Bureau of Public Affairs., 14 September 2007. https://2001-2009 .state.gov/r/pa/ho/time/jd/92068.htm.

58  Frederick C. Leiner, *The End of Barbary Terror: America's 1815 War against the Pirates of North Africa.* Oxford, New York: Oxford University Press, 2007. p. 175.

59  Deutsche Welle. 'East Africa's Forgotten Slave Trade | DW | 22.08.2019'. DW.COM. https://www.dw.com/en /east-africas-forgotten-slave-trade/a-50126759.

60  Lovejoy, Paul E. *Transformations in Slavery: A History of Slavery in Africa.* 3rd edn. Cambridge University Press, 2012. African Studies Book, p. 117; for a general history see Fage, J. D., John E. Flint, John Edgar Flint and Roland Anthony Oliver. *The Cambridge History of Africa.* Cambridge University Press, 1975.

61  Pétré-Grenouilleau, Olivier. *Les Traites Négrières: essaie d'histoire globale.* Paris: Gallimard, 2004, pp. 179–81; see also Mann, Kristin. *Slavery and the Birth of an African City: Lagos, 1760–1900.* Indiana University Press, 2007.

62  Thornton, John K. 'Slave Trade in the Atlantic World'. https:// www.gale.com/intl/essays/john-k-thornton-debates-over-slave

ry-abolition-slave-trade-atlantic-world; For more on this see his extensive *A Cultural History of the Atlantic World, 1250-1830*. Cambridge University Press, 2012.

63  Thornton, John K. *A Cultural History of the Atlantic World, 1250-1830*. Cambridge University Press, 2012, pp. 63–4.

64  Perbi, Akosua. 2001. 'Slavery and the Slave Trade in Pre-Colonial Africa.' Paper delivered at the University of Illinois. http://latin americanstudies.org/slavery/perbi.pdf.

65  Fuglestad, Finn. *Slave Traders by Invitation: West Africa's Slave Coast in the Precolonial Era*. Oxford: Oxford University Press, 2018.

66  Law, Robin. 'Dahomey and the Slave Trade: Reflections on the Historiography of the Rise of Dahomey'. *Journal of African History* 27 (2) (July 1986): 237–67; see also his '"My Head Belongs to the King": On the Political and Ritual Significance of Decapitation in Pre-Colonial Dahomey'. *Journal of African History* 30 (3) (November 1989): 399–415; for an analysis of early Dahomey political consolidation see his 'A Neglected Account of the Dahomian Conquest of Whydah (1727): The "Relation de La Guerre de Juda" of the Sieur Ringard of Nantes'. *History in Africa* 15 (1988): 321–38; for a more general outline of pre-colonial African polities see Monroe, J. Cameron. 'Power and Agency in Precolonial African States'. *Annual Review of Anthropology* 42 (1) (21 October 2013): 17–35.

67  Law, Robin. 'The Politics of Commercial Transition: Factional Conflict in Dahomey in the Context of the Ending of the Atlantic Slave Trade'. *Journal of African History*, 38 (1997): 213–33.

68  PBS NewsHour. 'How the West Got Rich and Modern Capitalism Was Born', 13 February 2015. https://www.pbs.org/newsh our/nation/west-got-rich-modern-capitalism-born;  See his extended discussion Beckert, Sven. *Empire of Cotton: A Global History*. 1st edn. New York: Knopf, 2014; for the classic statement of this see Williams, Eric Eustace. *Capitalism & Slavery*. 1st edn. Chapel Hill: University North Carolina Press, 1994; see also Findlay, Ronald and Kevin H. O'Rourke. *Power and Plenty:*

*Trade, War, and the World Economy in the Second Millennium.* Princeton University Press, 2009; Blackburn, Robin. *The Making of New World Slavery: From the Baroque to the Modern, 1492–1800.* Verso, 1998. For an incisive critique see Burnard, Trevor and Giorgio Riello. 'Slavery and the New History of Capitalism'. *Journal of Global History* 15 (2) (July 2020): 225–44.

69  Khan, Imran. 'Britain Was Built on the Backs, and Souls, of Slaves'. https://www.aljazeera.com/features/2020/6/11/britain -was-built-on-the-backs-and-souls-of-slaves.

70  Hirsch, Afua. 'The Case for British Slavery Reparations Can No Longer Be Brushed Aside'. *Guardian*, 9 July 2020; Chappell, Kate and Brian Ellsworth. 'British Royals' Jamaica Visit Stirs Demands for Slavery Reparations'. *Reuters*, 23 March 2022.

71  Engerman, Stanley L. 'The Slave Trade and British Capital Formation in the Eighteenth Century: A Comment on the Williams Thesis'. *Business History Review* 46 (4) (1972): 430–43. https://doi.org/10.2307/3113341.

72  'Legacies of British Slavery'. https://www.ucl.ac.uk/lbs//.

73  'Office of Registry of Colonial Slaves and Slave Compensation Commission: Records'. Volume(s), 1851 1812. T 71. The National Archives, Kew.

74  *Independent.* 'Britain's Colonial Shame: Slave-Owners given Huge Payouts After', 26 February 2013.

75  McCloskey, Deirdre Nansen. *Bourgeois Dignity: Why Economics Can't Explain the Modern World.* Chicago, IL: University of Chicago Press, 2011.

76  Mokyr, Joel. 'Editor's Introduction: The New Economic History and the Industrial Revolution', in *The British Industrial Revolution* (2nd edn). Routledge, 1999; chapter in full here https://cpb-us -e1.wpmucdn.com/sites/northwestern.edu/dist/3/1222/files/20 16/06/Editors-Introduction-The-New-Economic-History-1999 -1thoner.pdf.

77  Eltis, David and Stanley L. Engerman. 'The Importance of Slavery and the Slave Trade to Industrializing Britain'. *Journal of Economic History* 60 (1) (March 2000): 130.

78  Ibid., p. 135.
79  Thomas, Robert Paul. 'The Sugar Colonies of the Old Empire: Profit or Loss for Great Britain?' *Economic History Review* 21 (1) (1968): 30–45, p. 30.
80  For a summary, CEPR. 'Accounting for the Great Divergence'. https://cepr.org/voxeu/columns/accounting-great-divergence; for a fuller exposition see the excellent Broadberry, Stephen, Bruce M. S. Campbell, Alexander Klein, Mark Overton and Bas van Leeuwen. *British Economic Growth, 1270–1870*. Cambridge University Press, 2015.
81  'The National Archives | Exhibitions | Citizenship | Struggle for Democracy'. https://www.nationalarchives.gov.uk/pathways/citizenship/struggle_democracy/getting_vote.htm.
82  'British Navy Impressment | History Detectives | PBS'. https://www.pbs.org/opb/historydetectives/feature/british-navy-impressment/.
83  'How Has Life Expectancy Changed over Time? – Office for National Statistics'. https://www.ons.gov.uk/peoplepopulationandcommunity/birthsdeathsandmarriages/lifeexpectancies/articles/howhaslifeexpectancychangedovertime/2015-09-09.
84  'Testimony Gathered by Ashley's Mines Commission'. https://victorianweb.org/history/ashley.html.
85  BBC News. 'Fulbourn Blue Plaque Planned to Honour Chimney Sweep', 27 February 2022. https://www.bbc.com/news/uk-england-cambridgeshire-60548227.
86  'The New Poor Law'. https://www.workhouses.org.uk/poorlaws/newpoorlaw.shtml.

## 5 Accounting for 'wokery'

1  'Understanding Society – The UK Household Longitudinal Study'. https://www.understandingsociety.ac.uk/.
2  Asthana, Anushka. 'Muslims Are Truest of True Brits, Claims Study into National Sense of Belonging'. https://www.thetimes.co.uk/article/muslims-are-truest-of-true-brits-claims-study-into-national-sense-of-belonging-lv6lkvtlqhd.

3  Mohdin, Aamna. 'UK Universities Are Institutionally Racist, Says Leading Vice-Chancellor'. *Guardian*, 28 April 2021.

4  Sowell, Thomas. *Discrimination and Disparities*. Hachette UK, 2019.

5  Tobin, Sam. 'Students at University of Kent Must Take "White Privilege" Course'https://www.thetimes.co.uk/article/students -at-university-of-kent-must-take-white-privilege-course-clc9z m6nl.

6  Bloom, Dan. 'Teachers Who Use Term "White Privilege" Should Be Reported as Extremists Says MP'. *Mirror*, 9 October 2021. https://www.mirror.co.uk/news/politics/teachers-who-use-te rm-white-25170893.

7  BBC News. 'Black Lives Matter: Sir Keir Starmer "Regrets" Calling Movement a "Moment"', 2 July 2020.

8  GOV.UK. 'The Report of the Commission on Race and Ethnic Disparities'. https://www.gov.uk/government/publications/the -report-of-the-commission-on-race-and-ethnic-disparities.

9  Mos-Shogbamimu, Shola [@SholaMos1]. 'Racist Boris Johnson "Race Commission" Fronted by Token Black Man, Tony Sewell, Finds Institutional Racism Doesn't Exist'. A #WhiteSupremacy LIE to Gaslight Entire Nation #ThisIsWhyIResist Britain. Is. Not. A. Model. Of. Racial. Equality.#BlackLivesMatter Https://T.Co /Kl2ckrZ8HJ'. Tweet. *Twitter*, 31 March 2021. https://twitter .com/SholaMos1/status/1377156395842248704.

10 Courea, Eleni, Correspondent and Political Reporter and Henry Zeffman, Chief Political. 'Race Review Chief Tony Sewell Compared to Joseph Goebbels in Social Media Abuse'. https:// www.thetimes.co.uk/article/race-review-chief-tony-sewell-com pared-to-joseph-goebbels-in-social-media-abuse-hrww2whww.

11 WonkHE. 'W Is for Whiteness in Higher Education'. https://won khe.com/blogs/w-is-for-whiteness-in-higher-education/.

12 Ehsen, Rakib and Doug Stoges. 'Poor White Men and Labour's Identity Trap', *Critic Magazine*, 30 April 2021.

13 Chappell, Elliot. 'Labour Launches Forums to Inform "Race Equality Act Shaped by Lived Experience"'. LabourList. https://

labourlist.org/2021/05/labour-launches-forums-to-inform-race
-equality-act-shaped-by-lived-experience/.

14  Ibid.
15  Rule Book | The Labour Party. https://labour.org.uk/rulebook.
16  *Time*. 'She Coined the Term "Intersectionality" Over 30 Years Ago. Here's What It Means to Her Today'. https://time.com/5786710/kimberle-crenshaw-intersectionality/;   for her original exposition see Crenshaw, Kimberlé. 'Demarginalizing the Intersection of Race and Sex: A Black Feminist Critique of Antidiscrimination Doctrine, Feminist Theory and Antiracist Politics'. *University of Chicago Legal Forum* 140 (1989): 139–67.
17  Stahl, Ashley. '3 Benefits of Diversity in the Workplace'. *Forbes*.
18  Putnam, Robert D. 'E Pluribus Unum: Diversity and Community in the Twenty-First Century. The 2006 Johan Skytte Prize Lecture'. *Scandinavian Political Studies* 30 (2) (2007): 137–74.
19  Thomson Reuters Institute. 'How to Address DEI Concerns of White Men Who Feel They're Being Disadvantaged', 30 September 2022.
20  'Black Bristol Scholarship Programme'. University of Bristol. https://www.bristol.ac.uk/students/support/finances/scholarships/black-bristol-scholarship-programme/.
21  'Bursaries and Scholarships'. University of Bristol. https://www.bristol.ac.uk/students/support/finances/scholarships/.
22  *Independent*. 'Cambridge Academic Says She Will Not Work for University after Accusing Porters of Racist Abuse', 21 June 2018. https://www.independent.co.uk/news/education/education-news/cambridge-academic-strike-racism-porters-doctor-priyamvada-gopal-english-a8407981.html.
23  Steele, Shelby. *White Guilt: How Blacks and Whites Together Destroyed the Promise of the Civil Rights Era*. HarperCollins, 2009, pp. 62–3.
24  Ibid., p. 65.
25  Associated Press. 'California Group Votes to Limit Reparations to Slave Descendants'. *NPR*, 30 March 2022.

26  Woodson, Robert L. Sr. *Red, White, and Black: Rescuing American History from Revisionists and Race Hustlers*. Emancipation Books, 2021; for an earlier and acerbic exposition see also Stanley Crouch. *The All-American Skin Game, Or Decoy of Race: The Long and the Short of It, 1990–1994*. Knopf Doubleday Publishing Group, 1997. See also Harold Cruse. 'The Crisis of the Negro Intellectual: A Historical Analysis of the Failure of Black Leadership'. *New York Review Books*, 2005.

27  Wesley Yang [@wesyang]. '"Successor Ideology" in Its Bland but Vaguely Minatory Non-Specificity May Be the Correct Term for the Melange of Academic Radicalism Now Seeking Hegemony throughout American Institutions. It's My Own Coinage, but Perhaps Others Will Adopt It'. Tweet. *Twitter*, 25 May 2019. https://twitter.com/wesyang/status/1132128661556142080.

28  Douthat, Ross. 'Opinion | The Rise of Woke Capital'. *New York Times*, 28 February 2018, sec. Opinion. https://www.nytimes .com/2018/02/28/opinion/corporate-america-activism.html.

29  Sorkin, Andrew Ross, Bernhard Warner, Vivian Giang, Sarah Kessler, Stephen Gandel, Michael J. de la Merced, Lauren Hirsch and Ephrat Livni. 'An Anti-E.S.G. Activist Takes on Apple and Disney'. *New York Times*, 20 September 2022, sec. Business. https://www.nytimes.com/2022/09/20/business/dealbook/anti -esg-campaign-fund-etf-disney-apple.html.

30  Rapoza, Kenneth. 'Disney Forced To Face Activist Shareholder Inquiring About China'. *Forbes*. March 11, 2022.

31  BBC News. 'UK Universities Comply with China's Internet Restrictions', 9 July 2020.

32  Williams, Ian. 'How China Bought Cambridge. *Spectator*.

33  *WSJ*. 'The Successor Ideology and the Threat to Our Freedoms – Opinion: Free Expression – WSJ Podcasts'. https://www.wsj .com/podcasts/opinion-free-expression/the-successor-ideology -and-the-threat-to-our-freedoms/af093a5e-4f8e-4697-a406-ac0 6673f09b2.

34  Kaufman, Eric. 'The Politics of the Culture Wars in Contemporary America', 20 January 2022. Manhattan Institute. https://www

.manhattan-institute.org/kaufmann-politics-culture-war-con temporary-america; Doyle, Andrew. *The New Puritans: How the Religion of Social Justice Captured the Western World*. Hachette UK, 2022.

35 *Economist*. 'The Great Awokening – America's Threat from the Illiberal Left'. https://www.economist.com/podcasts/2021/09/03/the-great-awokening-americas-threat-from-the-illiberal-left.

36 McWhorter, John. *Woke Racism: How a New Religion Has Betrayed Black America*. Swift Press, 2021; see also Doyle, Andrew. *The New Puritans: How the Religion of Social Justice Captured the Western World*. Hachette UK, 2022.

37 Yang, Wesley [@wesyang]. 'It's a Kind of Authoritarian Utopianism That Masquerades as Liberal Humanism While Usurping It from within.' Tweet. *Twitter*, 25 May 2019. https://twitter.com/wesyang/status/1132130408794066944.

38 Bouie, Jamelle. 'The Enlightenment's Dark Side'. *Slate*, 5 June 2018.

39 Sensoy, Özlem and Robin DiAngelo. *Is Everyone Really Equal?: An Introduction to Key Concepts in Social Justice Education*. Teachers College Press, 2017, p. 5.

40 Delgado, Richard and Jean Stefancic. *Critical Race Theory: An Introduction*. New York University Press, 2012, p. 7.

41 *First Things*. 'Replace the Elite | Patrick J. Deneen'. https://www.firstthings.com/article/2020/03/replace-the-elite; see Francis, Samuel T. *Power and History: The Political Thought of James Burnham*. University Press of America, 1984. On the PMCs see Ehrenreich, John; Barbara Ehrenreich (1979). Pat Walker (ed.), *Between Labor and Capital* (1st edn). Boston: South End Press.

42 Liu, Catherine. *Virtue Hoarders: The Case against the Professional Managerial Class*. University of Minnesota Press, 2021; See also 'Virtue Hoarders: Our Scolding Elites'. https://www.spiked-online.com/2021/01/21/virtue-hoarders-our-scolding-elites/; Goodhart, David. *The Road to Somewhere: The New Tribes Shaping British Politics*. UK, USA, Canada, Ireland, Australia, India, New Zealand, South Africa: Penguin, 2017.

43 Deneen, Patrick J. *Why Liberalism Failed*. Yale University Press, 2019, p. 132.

44 Lasch, Christopher. *The Revolt of the Elites and the Betrayal of Democracy*. W. W. Norton & Company, 1996, p. 29.

45 Lind, Michael. *The New Class War: Saving Democracy from the Metropolitan Elite*. Atlantic Books, 2020; in the UK context see Embery, Paul. *Despised: Why the Modern Left Loathes the Working Class*. John Wiley & Sons, 2020.

46 Diaz, Daniella and Jessica Dean. 'McCarthy Calls on Biden to Apologize after "semi-Fascism" Remark'. *CNN*. https://www .cnn.com/2022/09/01/politics/kevin-mccarthy-speech-biden/in dex.html; Matt Zarb-Cousin. 'In Defence of Calling White Men "Gammon"'. Huck Magazine, 7 February 2018. https://www.hu ckmag.com/perspectives/opinion-perspectives/defence-calling -people-gammon/.

47 Goldberg, Zach [@ZachG932]. '1/n If 2016 Was the Year White Liberals Started Rating Non-Whites More Warmly than Whites, 2020 Was the Year They Started. (a) Rating Whites as More Violent than Blacks. https://T.Co/ZLiEFFh876'. Tweet. *Twitter*, 2 September 2022. https://twitter.com/ZachG932/status/156581 0798236155904.

48 Yglesias, Matthew. 'White Liberals Are Embracing Progressive Racial Politics and Transforming America'. *Vox*, 22 March 2019.

49 Lasch, Christopher. *The Revolt of the Elites and the Betrayal of Democracy (Revised) a Book by Christopher Lasch*. W. W. Norton & Company, 2011.

50 Lind, Michael. 'Britain's New Class War'. *UnHerd*, 5 February 2020.

51 *Guardian*. 'Biden Tells Voters "You Ain't Black" If You're Still Deciding between Him and Trump – Video', 22 May 2020, sec. US news. http://www.theguardian.com/us-news/video/2020 /may/22/joe-biden-charlamagne-you-aint-black-trump-video.

52 Crawford, Matthew. 'How Race Politics Liberated the Elites'. *UnHerd*, 14 December 2020.

53  Ibid.

54  Ramsay, Peter. 'Vulnerability as Ideology'. The Northern Star, 13 April 2022.

55  Furedi, Frank. 'The Therapeutic University'. *American Interest* (blog), 8 March 2017. https://www.the-american-interest.com /2017/03/08/the-therapeutic-university/.

**Conclusion: The future of the West?**

1  For a US archival summary, see Warner, Geoffrey. 'The United States and the Suez Crisis'. *International Affairs* 67 (2) (1 April 1991): 303–17. https://doi.org/10.2307/2620833; For a more general summary see Gorst, Anthony and Saul Kelly, eds. *Whitehall and the Suez Crisis*. London: Routledge, 2000.

2  For a masterful account of the development of the US postwar order, see Ikenberry, G. John. *After Victory: Institutions, Strategic Restraint, and the Rebuilding of Order After Major Wars*. Princeton University Press, 2001; for an incisive critique see Porter, Patrick. *The False Promise of Liberal Order: Nostalgia, Delusion and the Rise of Trump*. John Wiley & Sons, 2020.

3  Kataoka, Tetsuya. *Defending An Economic Superpower: Reassessing The US-Japan Security Alliance*. New York: Routledge, 2019. https://doi.org/10.4324/9780429033223.

4  'Global Britain in a Competitive Age: The Integrated Review of Security, Defence, Development and Foreign Policy', Cabinet Office, 16/03/2021, https://bit.ly/3vX8RGY (found: 24/05/2021).

5  Connor, Neil. 'China's Xi Jinping recalls national "humiliation" to Britain as he seeks to stir patriotism in Hong Kong', *Daily Telegraph*, 1 July 2017, https://www.telegraph.co.uk/news/2017 /07/01/chinas-xi-jinping-recalls-national-humiliation-britain-se eks/ (found: 24/05/2021).

6  Biggar, Nigel. *Colonialism: A Moral Reckoning*. Glasgow: William Collins, 2023, pp. 6–7.

7  Joske, Alex. 'The Party Speaks for You'. Australian Strategic Policy Institute. September 2022. http://www.aspi.org.au/report /party-speaks-you.

8 'United Front in Australia: How China Is Infiltrating Politics, Business, Universities Locally | News.Com.Au – Australia's Leading News Site'. https://www.news.com.au/finance/economy /australian-economy/china-is-infiltrating-australia-on-multiple -fronts-from-politics-to-business-via-its-powerful-and-covert -united-front-agency/news-story/9318c7799e540164dd0b985b9 e8969c2.

9 Raleigh, Helen. '3 Key Takeaways From The US–China Summit In Alaska'. *Federalist*, 23 March 2021. https://thefederalist.com /2021/03/23/3-key-takeaways-from-the-u-s-china-summit-in -alaska/.

10 'Alaska Talks to Be Remembered in History as a Landmark'. Editorial – *Global Times*. https://www.globaltimes.cn/page/202 103/1218891.shtml.

11 'Five Eyes Today's Axis of White Supremacy'. Editorial – *Global Times*'. https://www.globaltimes.cn/page/202102/1216338.shtml.

12 Aceves, William J. 'Virtual Hatred: How Russia Tried to Start a Race War in the United States'. 24 *Mich. J. Race & L.* 177 (2019): 179.

13 Lockhart, P. R. 'How Russia Exploited Racial Tensions in America during the 2016 Elections'. *Vox*, 17 December 2018. https://www .vox.com/identities/2018/12/17/18145075/russia-facebook-twit ter-internet-research-agency-race.

14 *TASS*. 'Western-Imposed Order Provides for Racist Division of World – Russia's Top Diplomat'. https://tass.com/politics/149 8943.

15 Al Mayadeen English. 'West Desire for Unipolar World Caused Geopolitical Crisis: Lavrov'. *Al Mayadeen English*, 27 July 2022. https://english.almayadeen.net/news/politics/west-desire-for -unipolar-world-caused-geopolitical-crisis:-l.

16 Roser, Max and Esteban Ortiz-Ospina. 'Global Extreme Poverty'. *Our World in Data*, 25 May 2019. https://ourworldindata.org/ex treme-poverty.

17 *Our World in Data*. 'Most of Us Are Wrong about How the World Has Changed (Especially Those Who Are Pessimistic

about the Future)'. https://ourworldindata.org/wrong-about-the
-world.

18   Vile, John R. 'Frederick Douglass'. https://www.mtsu.edu/first
-amendment/article/1763/frederick-douglass.

19   Crawford, Matthew. 'Covid Was Liberalism's Endgame'. *UnHerd*,
20 May 2022. https://unherd.com/2022/05/covid-was-liberalis
ms-endgame/.

20   West, Ed. 'The Tragedy of Telford's Girls'. Substack newsletter.
*Wrong Side of History* (blog), 26 October 2022. https://edwest
.substack.com/p/the-tragedy-of-telfords-girls?utm_medium=
email.

21   Brown, David. 'Ethnic Background of Child Abusers "Must Be
Recorded"', sec. news. https://www.thetimes.co.uk/article/ethn
ic-background-of-child-abusers-must-be-recorded-3lts6vqrs.

22   BBC News. 'LGBT School Lessons Protests Spread Nationwide',
16 May 2019, https://www.bbc.com/news/uk-england-48294017.

23   Paice, Edward. *Youthquake: Why African Demography Should
Matter to the World*. Head of Zeus Ltd, 2021.

24   BBC News. 'UK Net Migration Hits All-Time Record at 504,000',
24 November 2022. https://www.bbc.com/news/uk-63743259.

25   Telhami, Shibley and Stella Rouse. 'Poll Reveals White Americans
See an Increase in Discrimination against Other White People
and Less against Other Racial Groups'. *The Conversation.* http://
theconversation.com/poll-reveals-white-americans-see-an-in
crease-in-discrimination-against-other-white-people-and-less
-against-other-racial-groups-185278; for more data see Shibley
Telhami, 'American Attitudes on Race and Ethnicity'. May 2022.
https://criticalissues.umd.edu/sites/criticalissues.umd.edu/files
/American%20Attitudes%20on%20Race%20and%20Ethnicity.pdf.

26   Hussey, Ian and Jan De Houwer. 'Completing a Race IAT
Increases Implicit Racial Bias'. *PsyArXiv*, 19 November 2018.
https://doi.org/10.31234/osf.io/vxsj7.

27   Gallup Inc.. 'Concern About Race Relations Persists After Floyd's
Death'. Gallup.com, 19 May 2022. https://news.gallup.com/poll
/392705/concern-race-relations-persists-floyd-death.aspx.

28  'Race Relations: How Have Things Changed since the 2020 Black
    Lives Matter Protests? | YouGov'. https://yougov.co.uk/topics
    /politics/articles-reports/2021/05/25/race-relations-how-have
    -things-changed-2020-black-.
29  Goodwin, Matthew, Kaufmann Eric and Erik Gahner Larsen.
    'Asymmetric Realignment: Immigration and Right Party Voting'.
    *Electoral Studies* 80 (1 December 2022). https://doi.org/10.1016
    /j.electstud.2022.102551; see also Kustov, Alexander. 'Do Anti-
    Immigration Voters Care More? Documenting the Issue of the
    Importance of Asymmetry of Immigration Attitudes'. *British
    Journal of Political Science*, 21 October 2022, 1–10. https://doi
    .org/10.1017/S0007123422000369.

# Index

A grades
  increase in A-level 68
Abolition of the Slave Trade Act
  (1807) 94
abolitionist movement 94, 96, 100,
  110
academic freedom 14, 54, 84, 86–7
Access and Participation Plans 77
accreditation
  and Race Equality Charter 40
activists, placating of 120, 121
Advance HE 40, 53, 55, 78
  figures on BAME staff and
    students 59–61
  and microaggressions 73
  and Race Equality Charter (REC)
    40, 41, 45
  Staff Statistical Report (2021) 60
Advancing Racial Equity and
  Support for Underserved
  Communities Act 1–2
Africa
  'blame the West' narrative
    89–90
  and China 90–1
  and descent-based slavery 95

intra-African slavery 103
legacy of colonialism and linking
  of problems to 88–90
population growth 148
slavery in 97–103
African Americans see black
  Americans
Akel, Sofia 33
Akinbosede, Daniel 43
Althusser, Louis 21
Amos, Baroness 42, 46
Andrews, Kehinde 19, 30–1, 93
Ansari, Nazenin 121
anti-colonial movements 16–18
anti-racism 146
  abandoning of liberal forms of 2
  centrality of identity and new 2, 3
  cultural effects of new 3
  features of new 2–3, 33, 93, 125,
    131
  and virtue signalling 132–3
anti-semitism 66
anti-Western narrative 141–2
apartheid, intellectual 62–3
Arab world 26
Ashley, Lord 109

Asians
    degree attainment 64
    identification with Britishness 112
    see also BAME
Association for Promoting
    Abolition of Slavery 110
asylum seekers 11
Athena SWAN 41
attainment gap see degree
    attainment gap
authoritarian states 15, 141, 144–5,
    150
authoritarian Utopianism 125
authors
    including of global South authors
        in reading lists 48
Azumah, J. 99

Badenoch, Kemi 8
BAME (black, Asian or minority
    ethnic) staff/academics 43, 61
    Advance HE figures on 60–1
BAME (black, Asian or minority
    ethnic) students
    Advance HE figures on 61
    connecting with lived experiences
        of 44
    and curriculum 45
    and degree attainment gap 41–4,
        53, 64–5
    high educational outcomes 66
    lack of role models for 43
    over-representation of at select
        universities 69, 120
    university intake 9–10, 61
Barbary slave trade 99–100
BBC 8
Becker, Saul 43
Beckert, Sven 19
Bhambra, Gurminder K. 26
    Decolonising the University 28
Biden, President Joe 1–2, 126, 130,
        132, 143
Biggar, Nigel 142

binaries
    Derrida's theory of hierarchically
        organised 24–5, 26, 30, 82
bipolar world 140–1, 146
black Africans 9, 12, 65–6
    exclusion from school 65
    FSM progress to higher
        education/university 10, 65,
        77
    see also BAME
black Americans
    hate crimes committed by 6, 7
    killing of by police 4, 6
    killing of police by offenders 5, 7
    percentage of population 4
    as victims of crime 5
    as violent offenders statistics 5
black, Asian or minority ethnic see
    BAME
'black' category
    differences within 65
Black Death (1348) 107
Black, Jeremy 81, 96
Black Lives Matter see BLM
    movement
black students
    percentage of all first-year
        undergraduates 69
    and state schools 68
    university intake rates 9–10, 76
    see also BAME students
BlackRock 3
BLM movement 1, 3, 35, 49, 53,
        71–2, 93, 115, 149
BME see BAME
Brazil
    slave trade 96–7
Brewster, George 109
Brexit 11, 12, 130, 133, 140
Bristol University
    scholarship programme for black
        students 120
Britain 3–4, 7–12
    abolition of slavery and

compensation given to slave proprietors 104–5, 110
anti-discrimination norms and non-discriminatory nature of 8–10
attempts to end slavery/slave trade across the world 94, 96–7, 98, 102–3, 104, 110, 117
in a bipolar world 140–1
Brexit 11, 12, 130, 133, 140
child labour 108–9
and China 141–2
decolonial critique of history of 4, 19
economic enrichment and slavery allegation 103–7
heightening of inequality by slave trade 107
and iconoclasm 93
identification with 'Britishness' by ethnic minorities 112
immigration 8, 11, 29, 130, 148–9
impact of slave trade today 93
life of ordinary people during time of slavery 107–11
living conditions and life expectancy in nineteenth century 108–10
one of the least racist countries in the world 8, 9, 12, 112
protests against racial injustice in 3, 93
race relations after Floyd murder 149
relations with United States 105
and Second World War 138
and slave trade 32, 93–4
success of ethnic minorities in 12
sugar industry 106
universal suffrage 108
view of as racist 7–8, 12, 29, 113, 114–15
workhouses 109, 109–10
British Empire 81, 94, 105, 107, 110

British Future 112
British Police Service 12
British West Indies 105, 106
Bronstein, Edward 6
Bruckner, Pascal
    *The Tyranny of Guilt* 91
Buckingham, Professor Julia 36
Byrne, Ed 46

California 122
Cambridge University 73
    'Decolonise Sociology' 48–9
    relations with China's political elites 124
Cambridge University Library 49
Campbell, Bradley 72
Canterbury, Archbishop of 3
capitalism 19, 20, 30, 104
    movement away from class-based analysis of 21
    woke 122–6
Caribbean pupils
    FSM progression to higher education 10
    school exclusion of black 65
Caribbean slavery 105, 106
Castlereagh, Viscount 96
Centre for the Study of the Legacies of British Slavery 104
centre-Right 20
Charles, King 4
child labour 108–9
China 140, 141–3
    and Africa 90–1
    anti-Western sentiment 141–2
    and Britain 141–2
    cultural revolution 19
    loss of Hong Kong to Britain 142
    online students from 124
    role in African slavery 90–1
    strategy of exacerbating racial tension in the West 142–3
    United Front Work Department 142–3

China (*cont.*)
  and United States 143
  weaponising wokery to attack the
    West 142
Chinese academics 61
Chinese Communist Party (CCP)
  124, 142
Chinese employees
  earnings compared to British
    employees 10, 77–8
  median hourly pay 77–8
Chinese pupils
  FSM progression to higher
    education 10, 77
  university intake 10
Churchill, Winston 3
class 13, 79, 116
  and Marxism 20
  rejection of by poststructuralism
    21
  shifting to identity from 21, 114
class conflicts 20–1
class war 111, 114, 133
Clinton, Hilary 130
collective racial guilt 2, 33, 39, 79,
  103, 104, 107–8, 146
colonialism 13, 14, 18, 27, 32, 66, 81
  and British universities 28
  explaining wealth gap between
    West and the global South 32?
  linking of problems in Africa to
    88–9
  *see also* post-colonialism
colour blindness 52
Colston, Edward
  toppling of statue of 3, 104
Commission on Race and Ethnic
  Disparities (CRED) report
  (2021) 115–16
conceptual apartheid 62–3
Congress of Vienna 96
Cook, Mary Curnock 78
Corbyn, Jeremy 115
Cordova, Marsha de 115, 116

corporate virtue signalling 123
correspondence theory of
  knowledge 62–3, 119
counter-histories 80–1
Crawford, Matthew 132–3
Crenshaw, Kimberlé 117
critical race theory/theorists (CRT)
  2, 29, 35, 42, 80, 147
critical social theory 21
Cromwell, Oliver 3, 100
cultural liberalism 124
cultural socialism 124–5
cultural story 136–7
culture, centrality of and
  postmodern focus on 13, 20–3,
  24, 31
culture wars 15, 125, 133, 137
curriculum
  and BAME students 45
  decolonisation of 39, 41, 45–50
  Eurocentric 13, 46, 47, 49, 50, 64,
    84
  exploring of 'indigenous
    worldviews' 47–8, 50
  reading lists 33, 39, 46, 48
  and NUS's campaign 43–4, 45

Dahomey, Kingdom of 102–3
Dallali, Shaima 66
Dandridge, Nicola 36
Danegeld tax 123
De Montfort University 47
degree attainment gap 41–4, 60,
  64–8
  accounting for by racism 53, 64,
    65–6, 68
  areas of improvement 44
  'black' category 65–6
  correlation between A-level
    results and degree outcome 64
  and degree choice 69
  and gender 78
  lack of role models for BAME
    students 43

NUS's curriculum campaign 43–4
response to by universities 43
and socio-economic class 68
statistics/data on 64
UUK report and recommendations 41–3, 44
variables explaining 67–70
degree choice
and degree attainment gap 69
Delgado, Richard 80
Deneen, Patrick J. 129
dependency theory 18
Derrida, Jacques 22, 24–5, 26, 31, 81, 82
DiAngelo, Robin 126
diversification 33
diversity 59–61, 75, 118
    alleged lack of among students and staff 59–60
    as a form of performative social justice 122
    and intersectionality 118
    and opinion 118
    problems with 118–19, 122
    and teacher–student relationship 62–3
    trend toward greater diversity in universities 60–1
Doku, Amatey 42
domestic norms 137–8
Douglass, Frederick 145
Dutch West India Company 101

EDI (Equality, Diversity, Inclusion) 2, 88
EDI bureaucracies 71–2, 73, 74
EDI committees 41
Edinburgh University
    and microaggressions 52
Education Select Committee 10–11
EHRC (Equality and Human Rights Commission) 35–7, 50–1, 52–3, 54, 70

analysis of reports on racism in universities 55–7
examples of mathiness in reports 58–9
promotion of moral panic through reports on racism 54, 55–7
report on microaggressions 50–1, 73
reports on racism (2019) 36–7
Ehrenreich, Barbara and John 127
Eltis, David 105
emotive reasoning 57, 70–5
Engerman, Stanley L. 105
Enlightenment 32, 80, 146
epistemological relativism 86
epistemology 22, 82, 83 see also knowledge
equality
    and Race Equality Charter 40–1
Equality Act (2010) 51, 52, 72
Equality, Diversity and Inclusion see EDI
ethnic employees
    higher median hourly rates than whites 77–8
ethnic minorities
    and degree attainment gap 41–4
    identification with 'Britishness' 112
    number of university students 55
    views on racial harassment by students and tackling of by universities 56
    see also BAME
EU (European Union)
    Discrimination in the European Union report (2019) 8
    expansion of 139
Eurocentric curriculum 13, 46, 47, 49, 50, 64, 84
Eurocentric narcissism 91
Eurocentrism 27, 81, 87–93

Europe 91, 139
and post-war US security 139
European Union Agency for
Fundamental Rights study
(2016) 9
Exeter University 46–7
'eye of the beholder' theory of
racism 71

Fair, Laura 98
Fanon, Frantz 31
*The Wretched of the Earth* 18
'fat acceptance movement' 84
finite population correction 58
'Five Eyes' intelligence 143
Floyd, George, killing of (2020) 1, 3,
4, 12, 35, 53, 72, 115, 149
Fodio, Usman dan 98
forced labour 95
forced marriage 95
Foucault, Michel 22–4, 26, 31, 81–2
France
abolition of slave trade 96
and process of decolonisation 17
Frankfurt School 20
Free School Meal (FSM) status 10,
11, 65, 76–7
freedom 147
academic 14, 54, 84, 86–7
French poststructuralism 20
Friend–enemy distinction 147
Furedi, Frank 134

Gandhi, Mahatma 3
Gavaghan, David 43
gender 78
gender disparities 114
gender participation rates 78
gender self-identification
and social constructivism 84
Germany 140
Ghezo, King 102
Gladstone, John 105
Gladstone, William 105

global South authors
including of in reading lists 48
*Global Times* 143
globalisation 131
and the managerial class 127–30
Goldsmiths University 43
Gooder, Sarah 109
Goodhart, David 128
Gopal, Professor Priyamvada 48–9,
115
Grady, Jo 26, 50
Gramsci, Antonio 20
grievance 13, 63, 112, 150
politics of 122, 131, 132, 133
*Guardian* 37
Guess, Teresa 29–30
guilt 142
historical 147
*see also* collective racial guilt

Hancock, Matt 74
Harris, Kamala 2
Hastings, Lord 139
hate crimes 6, 7
hierarchies 82
Derrida's theory of 24–5, 26, 30,
82
Higher Education Policy Institute
(HEPI) 49–50, 78
Higher Education Statistics Agency
(HESA) 64
Hilsenrath, Rebecca 36
historical arguments
and decolonisation 14, 80–111
historical guilt 147
historical narratives 136
Hobbes, Thomas 140
homosexuality 81–2
Hong Kong 66
China's loss of to Britain 142
human rights 129
Huskar mining Colliery (Silkstone)
109
Hutcheon, Linda 25–6

Ibori, James 89
ICM Unlimited 11
ideas
    centrality of 21–2, 24, 31
    shared 23
identity 114
    centrality of 2, 3, 13, 21–2, 114
    wokery's emphasis on 125–6
identity diversity 118
identity politics 15, 16–34, 25, 32, 81,
    116, 117, 120
illiberalism
    intersectional 117–22
    in universities 54–79
immigration/immigrants
    and Britain 11, 29, 130, 149
Imperial College
    and microaggressions 52
Independent Inquiry into Child
    Sexual Abuse 148
India
    caste system 95
    slave population 95
'indigenous worldviews' 47–8, 50
Industrial Revolution 105, 106
intake, university
    black students 76
    BME 9–10, 61
    and gender 78
    white working-class students 63,
    76, 77, 79, 126
intersectional illiberalism 117–22
intersectionality 117, 118–19, 122–3,
    135
Iran, revolution (1979) 2
Islamic slave trade 97, 98–9, 101,
    103
Italy 8

Japan 118, 139
Jews 66–7
John Schofield Trust 121
Johns, Alison 59–60
judgemental rationalism 86

judgemental relativism 13, 24, 83–5,
    86

Kandola, Professor Binna
    Racism at Work 74
Kaufman, Eric 124–5
Keele University, Decolonise
    network 46
Khrushchev, Nikita 16
King, Martin Luther 1, 2
King's College London 46, 47
    'indigenous initiative' 47
    race equality action plan 51
Kissinger, Henry 142
knowledge
    correspondence theory of 62–3,
    119
    and power 23, 26, 81
    social constructivist theory of 22,
    81

Labour party 116
    commitment to introducing new
        Race Equality Act 116
    reaction to CRED report 116
    view that British society is racist
        114–15, 116
Lamberts, Koen 51–2
Lasch, Christopher 129, 131
Lavrov, Russian Foreign Minister
    144
Left social theory 13, 16–22
Lewis, Clive 116
liberal international order 15, 135,
    136–9
liberalism, cultural 124
Lin Biao 17–18
Lind, Michael 129
Liu, Catherine 128
Liverpool University
    unconscious bias training 51
Lodhi, Abdulazizi 100
London Metropolitan 69
Lovejoy, Paul E. 101

McWhorter, John 125
madness
    Foucault on 23–4
Makaula, Siyanda 87
Maldonado-Torres, Nelson et al.
    33
managerial class
    and globalisation 127–30
    and moral panic 131
    see also PMC (Professional
    Managerial Class)
Manning, Jason 72
Marcuse, Herbert 20
Marxism 20–1, 122–3
    decline in popularity and failure
    of revolutionary 13, 17, 19–20,
    31
    see also post-Marxist theory
Masino, Serena 47
mathematics
    and mathiness 58–9
mathiness 58–70
maths curriculum 87
media
    racist narrative and UK 7–8
    racist narrative and US 6, 7
mental illness
    Foucault on 23–4
microaggressions, racial 39, 41,
    50–2, 53, 70–5, 85
    definition 50
    as emotive reasoning 71
    examples of 52, 73–4
    and mind-reading 71
    university responses to 51–2
migration 8, 131, 148–9
mind independence 86, 88
    and scientific realism 85–6
mind-reading 71
mission statements 45–6
Mokyr, Joel 105
moral panic 54–79, 113, 134
    and EDI bureaucracies 71–2
    mathiness 58–9

microaggressions and emotive
    reasoning 70–5
and Munchausen syndrome by
    progressive proxy 131–5
negative consequences of 54
and PMC 131
promotion of by EHRC reports
    on racism in universities 54,
    55–7
and victimhood culture 72
weaponisation of by activists 71–2
and white working-class students
    76–8
moral relativism 25
Mos-Shogbamimu, Dr Shola 115
Moshiri, Azadeh 121
Moshiri, Farhad 121
MSOR (Mathematics, Statistics and
    Operational Research) 87
multiculturalism 148
multinational corporations
    adopting of woke capitalism
    123–4
multivariate analysis 67, 70
Munchausen syndrome by
    progressive proxy 131–5
Muslims
    identification with Britishness 112
'Myth of Meritocracy' 52

naive realism 86
Nandi, Alita 9
National Union of Students see
    NUS
NATO (North Atlantic Treaty
    Organization) 139, 140
Nelson, Horatio 3
NEON report 77
New History of Capitalism 19
Newsom, Gavin 122
Nigeria 89
Nigerian nationals
    visas granted to 11
Nobel Prize winners 67

non-aligned movement 16
non-Western histories 91, 92
North Atlantic Treaty Organization
    see NATO
NUS (National Union of Students)
    'Why Is My Curriculum White'
    campaign 43–4, 45

obesity 84
objectivity 24
    and postmodernism 24
    rejection of by decolonial critique
    32
    rejection of by social
    constructivists 81
OECD 140
Office for National Statistics (ONS)
    69
Office for Students 36
Okowa, Ifeanyi 89
ontological realism 86
ontology, importance of 82, 83–7
open enquiry 86–7
'open international order' 141
Open University 47
opinion
    and diversity 118
Orientalism 26, 27, 92
'othering' 25
Ottoman Empire 92, 100
Oxford University 43
    Black Academic Futures
    programme 43
    BME/BAME student intake 10, 61

Perbi, Akosda 101
philosophy, as bastion of whiteness
    33
Platt, Lucinda 9
PMC (Professional Managerial
    Class) 14, 127–30, 133–4
police (UK)
    and anti-racism 12
    BME confidence in 12

police/policing (US)
    anti-black racism in 4
    bias narrative in relation to 6
    black men killed by and media
    reporting on 4, 6
    interaction with citizens 5
    numbers killed by felons 5, 7
    political elites 28–9, 101, 104, 107,
    124
polytechnics 70
populism 129, 130, 133
Portugal
    and slave trade 106
positive racial discrimination 59
post-colonialism 25–7, 82
post-Marxist theory
    and decolonisation 22–5
postmodernism/postmodernists
    22, 31, 80
    and Foucault 22–5
    and judgemental relativism
    83
    and post-colonialism 25–6
    and social constructivism 22–3,
    81
    and truth 24, 31–2
poststructuralism, identity politics
    and French 20–1
poverty
    decline in world 145
power
    and knowledge 23, 26, 81
prejudice(s) 9, 14, 29
    and BBC 8
    unconscious 4
Prescod-Weinstein, Chanda 87
press gangs 108
Professional Managerial Class see
    PMC
progressives 27, 92, 110, 113, 122,
    123, 130, 147, 149–50
Public Sector Equality Duty (PSED)
    51, 72
Puri, Samir 92

Quality Assurance Agency 87
Quijano, Aníbal 27

race conflicts 21
Race Equality Charter (REC) 40–1,
  45–6, 59, 61–2
Racial Harassment Inquiry: A
  Survey of Universities 58
racial harassment incidents
  number reported in universities
    55–6, 58
racism 1, 78
  accounting for degree attainment
    gap 53, 64, 65–6, 68
  Biden legislation to counter 1–2
  by consequence 29–30
  by intent 29–30
  'eye of the beholder' theory of 71
  microaggressions and
    unconscious biases 39, 41,
    50–2, 53, 70–5, 85
  structural 2, 6, 38, 39, 40, 49, 60,
    66, 70, 116, 121
  systemic 3, 30, 41, 50, 113, 115
  on university campuses and
    tackling of 35–53, 56–7, 78
Ramsay, Peter 134
Rankine, Claudia 2
rational adjudication 14, 80
rationalism, judgemental 86
reading lists 33, 39, 46
  inclusion of global South authors
    48
realism
  naive 86
  ontological 86
  scientific see scientific realism
reason, defending 81–2
relativism, judgemental 13, 24, 83–5,
  86
Representation of the People Act
  (1918) 108
revolutionary movements
  and Left social theory 16–22

Ribeiro-Addy, Bell 115, 116
Richardson, Professor David 38, 113
role models
  lack of for BAME students 43
Romer, Paul 58
Royal Navy
  and ending of slave trade 96–7
  use of press gangs 108
Russell Group 10, 61, 70
Russia 141
  invasion of Ukraine (2022) 94,
    137, 140
  weaponising of wokery 143–4
Rutazibwa, Olivia U. 27, 88–9

Said, Edward 26, 31, 92
St Andrews University 52
Salau, Bashir 99
Sartre, Jean-Paul 18
Sayer, Andrew 83
science
  defending and importance of
    81–7
scientific realism 14, 80, 83–7
  defining 85
  and importance of ontology 83
  and mind independence 85–6
scientists
  decolonial critique of 87
Scotland
  and suffrage 108
Second World War 17, 137, 138
sensitivity analysis 57
Sensoy, Özlem 126
Sewell, Dr Tony 115
shared ideas 23
Sheffield University
  mandatory equality training
    programmes 51
  microaggression monitors 51–2
Shilliam, Robbie 27, 28
Choat 28
Sino-British Joint Declaration
  (1984) 142

Skidmore, Chris 36
Slave Compensation Commission
  104
slave revolts 96, 103
Slave Trade Act (1845) 96
Slavery Abolition Act (1833) 94, 104
slavery/slave trade 1, 4, 13, 81, 92,
  93–111, 116
  in Africa 97–103
  allegation of making Britain rich
    through 103–7
  attempts by Britain to end world
    94, 96–7, 98, 102–3, 104, 110,
    117
  Barbary white 99–100
  campaign for reparations for
    descendants of 104
  as central to West's economic
    development 19, 32
  China's role in African 90–1
  claim that all white British
    citizens are collectively guilty
    for the sin of 14
  descent-based 95
  destruction of statues by
    protesters 93, 103
  ending/abolition of 94, 96–7, 103
  in human history 95–6
  important part of decolonial
    critique of West 93
  intra-African 101
  Islamic 97, 98–9, 101, 103
  and Kingdom of Dahomey 102–3
  legacy of and the West 91
  modern-day 95
  and non-European empires 92
  and Sokoto Caliphate 98–9
  transatlantic 4, 32, 89, 91, 93–4,
    96, 97
social constructivism 22–3, 25, 30,
  80, 81, 84, 88
  emphasis on epistemology/
    knowledge 22, 81. 82, 83
  features of 22–3, 83

and gender self-identification 84
  rejection of truth 81
  as threat to foundations of
    Western civilisation 84
social justice 2, 14, 28, 32, 46, 62, 72,
  83, 114, 121, 122, 123–6, 149
social media 128
socialism, cultural 124–5
Society for the Abolition of the
  Slave Trade 110
socio-economic class 119–20
  and degree attainment gap 68
Sokoto caliphate 98–9
Solent University 51
Soviet Union 16, 139, 140
  collapse of (1991) 20
Sowell, Thomas 113
Spain
  abolition of slave trade 96
staff see university staff
Stanford, Social Innovation Review 2
Starmer, Sir Keir 115, 116
Steele, Shelby 121–2
Stefanic, Jean 80
state schools
  university intake from 9–10, 76,
    77
structural racism 2, 6, 38, 39, 40, 49,
  60, 66, 70, 116, 121
successor ideology 123
Sue, Derald Wing 71
suffrage 108
sugar industry 105, 106
Sumner, Charles 100
Sunak, Rishi 8
supranationalism 128, 130, 132
Sussex University 43
systemic racism 2, 30, 41, 50, 113, 115

Táíwò, Olúfmi 88
Tanzania 98
teacher–student relationship 62
  and correspondence theory of
    knowledge 62–3

Third World
　West's economic hegemony due
　　to exploitation of argument
　　18–19, 54
Third-Worldism 16–17
Thomas-Greenfield, Linda 1, 3
Thornton, John K. 101
Tickell, Adam 43
Timpa, Tony 6
Tip, Tippu 97–8
training staff 39
tribalism 147
Troope, Stephen 73
Trump, Donald 133
truth 24, 86
　decentring of 21, 31
　and postmodernism 24, 31–2
　rejection of by social
　　constructivists 81

UK see Britain
UK Education Select Committee
　report (2021) 76–7
Ukraine
　Russian invasion of (2022) 94,
　　137, 140
unconscious biases 50–2
unconscious bias training 45
United States
　attempt to end Barbary slave
　　trade 100
　and China 143
　construction of a liberal
　　international order after
　　Second World War 138–9
　increase in power after Second
　　World War 138
　lack of diversity at top of
　　corporate America 2–3
　movement against slavery in 100
　Navy's new fealty pledge 2
　post-war security provided by 139
　race relations after Floyd murder
　　149

　relations with Britain 105
　see also police/policing (US)
University of Kent
　Centre for Indigenous and Settler
　　Colonial Studies 47–8
University of Westminster 47
universal suffrage 108
universities, British 13
　accusation of unequal outcomes
　　for ethnic minorities 13
　BAME/BME student intake 9–10,
　　61
　calling for anti-racist cultural
　　change by UUK 37, 38–40
　and Chinese students 124
　and colonialism 28
　and curriculum see curriculum
　decolonisation theory and 27–9,
　　33
　degree attainment gap see degree
　　attainment gap
　EHRC reports on racism in 35–7,
　　52–3, 55–7
　as key vectors of white supremacy
　　and racial privilege 28–9
　moral panic and illiberalism in 14,
　　54–79, 134
　number of racial harassment
　　incidents reported 55–6, 58
　political bias on campuses 27–8
　and Race Equality Charter 40–1
　racism on campus and tackling of
　　35–53, 56–7
　response to microaggressons
　　60–1
　trend towards greater diversity in
　　60–1
　and whiteness concept 28–9, 32
Universities UK see UUK
University of Cambridge Museums
　(UCM) 49
University and College Union
　(UCU) 36, 50
University of East London 69

University of Leicester 48
university staff 55
 and diversity 59, 60
University of West London 69
US–Japan Security Pact 139
UUK (Universities UK) 37, 38–40,
 54, 72
 *Black, Asian and Minority Ethnic
 Student Attainment in UK
 Universities* report 41–3
 and changing the curriculum
 45
 decolonisation agenda 55
 reports (2022) 44
 suggestions how to counter white
 domination 39
 *Tackling Racial Harassment in
 Higher Education* 37

victimhood culture 72
Vietnam War 17
Vikings 123
virtue signalling 120, 124
 and anti-racism 132–3
 corporate 123
visas, post-Brexit 11

Wallerstein, Immanuel 18–19
Wardle, Betty 109
West 150
 China's strategy of
 exacerbating racial tensions
 in 142–3,
 economic hegemony due to
 exploitation of Third World
 argument 18–19, 54
 and legacy of slavery 91
 wealth traceable to slavery and
 colonialism 93
West Africa Squadron 96, 97
West African Empire 98–9
West, Ed 147
West India 105
'white domination' 38, 40

UUK's suggestions on how to
 counter 39
white empiricism 87
white guilt 74, 121
white privilege 2, 39, 45, 110, 114,
 115, 147
white supremacy 2, 7–8, 63
white working class 76–8, 79
 median hourly rate compared
 with ethnic employees 77–8
 white progressives hostility
 towards in US 130
white working-class pupils 63,
 76–8, 79, 121
 disadvantages of 10–11, 113
 and FSM 76–7
 under representation of in
 universities and reasons for 63,
 76, 77, 79, 126
whiteness 2, 28–31, 32, 33, 53, 79, 87,
 107, 110, 126
whiteness studies 29
woke capitalism 122–6
wokery 54, 111, 112–35, 145
 dangers of 145–7
 emphasis on identity 125
 as form of authoritarian
 Utopianism 125
 globalisation and the managerial
 class 127–30
 and interactional illiberalism
 117–22
 Munchausen syndrome by
 progressive proxy 131–5
 rejection and opposition to
 liberal norms 125–6
 secular religiosity of 125
 values seeking to deconstruct
 145
 weaponising of by China 142–3
 weaponising of by Russia
 143–4
*Woman King, The* (film) 103
WonkHE 38–9, 115–16

Woodson, Robert 122
workhouses 109–10
working class
    lack of class consciousness
        among 20
    *see also* white working class
world-systems analysis 18–19
Wyatt, Don 91

Xi Jinping 142, 143

Yang Jiechi 143
Yang, Wesley 122–3, 124
Yglesias, Matthew 125, 130

Zanzibar, and slave trade 97, 98
'zero-sum game mentality' 119